The Host With The Most

The Host With The Most

Tales Of A Tattooed Television Personality

Todd Newton

Copyright © 2016 Todd Newton
All rights reserved.

ISBN-13: 9781523959501
ISBN-10: 1523959509

For my children, with love. Thank you for adding so many beautiful colors to my life.

"Show me a man with a tattoo and I'll show you a man with an interesting past." -Jack London

Table of Contents

Introduction · xi

Chapter 1   A Fifth Grade Nightmare · 1
Chapter 2   And Here's Your Host · 12
Chapter 3   Make the Moment Matter · 26
Chapter 4   Who Are You Supposed To Be? · · · · · · · · · · · · · · · · · · 41
Chapter 5   Services Rendered. Pay the Man · · · · · · · · · · · · · · · · · 46
Chapter 6   That's My Boy · 66
Chapter 7   What eBay Taught Me About Life · · · · · · · · · · · · · · · · 76
Chapter 8   Tattooed in Hell · 85
Chapter 9   You Can't Go Out There Alone · · · · · · · · · · · · · · · · · 101
Chapter 10 Confessions of a Pizza Delivery Boy · · · · · · · · · · · · · · 118
Chapter 11 No Photography in the White House · · · · · · · · · · · · · 130
Chapter 12 Twenty Years Too Late · 143

Afterword · 149

Introduction

STANDING IN THE shadows of the stage wings, I tugged sharply at the crisp, white cuffs of my shirt protruding an inch below the sleeves of my pinstripe jacket. The royal blue cuff links recently purchased on a trip to Sweden caught the fading light of the house manager's small desk lamp. The Windsor knot of my lavender tie was tight around a neck freshly shaved by my barber's classic straight razor. My black dress shoes held a shine that would have made a Marine Corps drill sergeant stand at attention. I smiled at the feel of the newest addition to my on-stage attire; a gaudy pinky ring reminiscent of the old school Vegas performers that I so greatly admired and longed to emulate.

If there was one secret to whatever degree of success I may have achieved in my hosting career, it was that my entire outfit cost less than $500.

I am The Host with the Most®. The name was first bestowed upon me in 2006 by *Las Vegas Magazine* and has appeared in numerous publications and blogs ever since. Though I am not the first to be referred to as such, I will be the last because the moniker is now mine. Just as surely as you own the shoes on your feet, I own the title The Host with the Most®. Should you wish to verify this fact, you may find it in black and white on the United States Trademark and Patent Office website. Finders keepers.

I am the host with the most passion. I am the host with the most drive. And I am the host with the most respect for the art of hosting. My ambition may seem imposing and it is impossible to duplicate. My drive allows me to speak, write, and live with a degree of bravado that many would not be comfortable with. My vocation is not a stepping stone for me. It is not something I fell into after failing in another area. God did not speak to me and anoint me a host with bolts of lightning and horse-drawn chariots carrying trumpeters in flowing white robes, but it is my life's calling all the same.

The audience would never know, nor care, that my starched dress shirt and tie had been purchased at an outlet mall in South Florida. Nor would they ever suspect that the flashy cuff links that occasionally peek out at them from beneath my tailored jacket sleeves were indeed purchased in Sweden, but in a tourist-laden gift shop outside the gates of the Royal Palace. What of the dress shoes which were so polished that those sitting in the first three rows could see their own reflections? I acquired them by redeeming reward points and birthday coupons at the DSW in my local shopping mall. And the obnoxiously large ring weighing down my right hand is made of imitation gold and sprinkled with synthetic diamonds that I wipe down each night with a baby wipe. It, and three others of equal garishness, was purchased on eBay for less than twenty dollars.

My level of showmanship cannot be qualified as deceitful. I am not pretending to be something I am not. I am not acting nor am I lying to those who have chosen to open their wallets, taken off work, or hired a babysitter to attend tonight's presentation. What I am presenting is an authentic, yet slightly exaggerated, version of myself. Just in the same way we use filters to enhance the color of a photograph, I am simply amplifying those qualities within myself that I have used to entertain and inform for nearly thirty years. The audience expects the man or woman on stage to be flashier, have whiter teeth, and be more engaging than Average Joe or Plain Jane with whom they deal every day. After all, this is *show* business. And when it comes to the business of show, The Host with the Most® does not disappoint.

Exceeding the expectations of those seated just on the other side of the plush red curtain was my sole mission as I went through my silent pre-show rituals. I have always carried a worn photograph of my children in my left breast pocket during every engagement. Their faces are a constant reminder of why I do what I do. They represent the bigger picture in my life. While I am being introduced, I close my eyes and envision my beloved grandmother standing next to me. As I walk onto the stage, any stage, she pats me on my back the way she did when I was a child. My concentration is so intense that I can almost feel her hand on me. These deeply meaningful traditions put me in the perfect state of focus and poise. Whether it's a live game show, a corporate keynote presentation, or revealing the winner of a beauty pageant, I take my role of Master of Ceremonies as seriously as a surgeon who is preparing to enter the operating room. The stage is my office, the audience is my boss, and entertaining is what I am here to do.

Many have heard my story of responding to an ad in the St. Louis entertainment rag, *The Riverfront Times*. That small advertisement led to a gig hosting male dance revues all over the Midwest for $150 a week; quite a haul for a seventeen-year-old junior in high school. Now, decades later, my memories of the long car rides and the screaming women that took part in those shows have become blurred, but I can still recall the crunch of AquaNet hairspray in my hair and the bottom of my leather ankle boots sticking to the beer-soaked floors of the countless taverns and legion halls we performed in. The rush of adrenaline I experienced when that ideal concoction of verbiage departed my lips, was carried via sound waves through the microphone, and ultimately blasted through the sound system and was released into the nighttime air is as clear to me now as the honking of the taxis outside of my hotel room window. I learned early on in my career that a particular blend of syllables, perhaps something as simple as, "We've been waiting all year to get here to Peoria!" or "There's no place we need to be tomorrow so how 'bout we stay all night long with you, Memphis?" could incite near pandemonium with the bachelorettes and housewives desperate for a night out. It did not take long before I had mastered the art of driving these audience as if they were a luxury automobile. The stage became a heated leather seat which seemed tailored for my bottom and the microphone was my steering wheel. Once we all buckled ourselves in, there was no telling where the ride would take us.

It seems that everyone has an opinion on who and what makes a great host. Letterman, Conan, Fallon, Colbert, Kimmel, Dawson, Barker, we all have our favorites that make us feel as if we're in on the joke or, at least, a part of the conversation. For some unexplainable reason, there are no college courses on the subject, and there has never been a book written on the art of hosting by someone who came up through the trenches doing it. I can't pinpoint a single book where a man who feeds his family by standing before the masses and saying, "This is who and what I am. I hope you love it because it's all I've got," has filled the pages with the truth of what this career entails. The fact that young people are not given the opportunity to learn the art of highlighting the very best of themselves for financial gain is as ludicrous as the absence of courses on real world topics such as money management, interviewing for a job, or the art of negotiation. Instead, the professional host is left to fend for himself or herself. This book will show that my profession is one of highs and lows, green lights and cancelations, and accolades and criticisms. *The Host with the Most* is much more than a generic How To Guide on Hosting, it is your all access pass and a front row seat to what I know to be the greatest job in the world.

I'll state up front that the good times have far outweighed the bad. I've never shied away from working harder than most thought logical because I've always loved the grind. I still do. The entertainment industry is not all spotlights, town cars, and pretty women lining up to accompany you to award shows. It also consists of hours spent in airport lounges and microwave dinners eaten on the run. I've showered in truck stops and slept in train stations all to get where I needed to be and do what I needed to do. Somehow my stiff back and the bags under my eyes have always seemed to disappear once that little red light comes on. And age has not depleted my hustle. In fact, I work harder today than I ever have. Being a host is tougher now than it has ever been. At one point in my career, my agent would call with an audition. I'd drive to the location and see the same faces in the waiting in the lobby for their shot to read: JD Roberto, Mark Steines, Mark L. Walberg, Roger Lodge, Chris Hardwick, and Dave Holmes. We'd say our hellos and wish each other luck as one by one we went into display our goods to the casting director. The brotherhood we formed during those many outings allowed us to be happy for whichever guy ended up landing the gig.

But in the early 2000's, recognized celebrities began infiltrating our sacred circle, and the bigger names began landing the bigger jobs. Hosts at my level found ourselves residing in the world of basic cable television and corporate events while the major networks cashed in on the recently available star power. For me, cable was a wonderful and prosperous place to be. I've been able to build a healthy and respectable body of work without the ratings pressure that accompanies primetime network television.

Today the Internet offers sites like Periscope and YouTube that give anyone with a laptop and some free time the opportunity to introduce their show idea to the world. I am a firm believer that there is plenty of room in the marketplace for everyone, and no one should have their creativity stifled by the red tape of corporate greed. The focus must be on the content and the delivery. Those who build and maintain a brand will rise to the top. Fortunately for me, I've been given opportunity after opportunity to build for years.

Hosting is my craft. Some choose a career in music, acting, or comedy. Those who have no desire for the spotlight pursue medicine, philanthropic work, or are free to stay at home and devote all of their time and talents to raising children. I, however, did not deliberately choose this path. This glorious path chose me. The only "job" I've ever held was delivering pizzas in 1986, and you will soon see how that saga played out. Since slinging that last pie, I have never felt as if I had to work for a living. That's been another secret of mine. I cannot imagine wasting even a single day in a job that wasn't pointing me in the direction I wanted my life to go. None of us have the luxury of looking into a crystal ball and seeing how many tomorrows we've been given, so why not take this ride for all it's worth? Spinning your wheels at a job or in a relationship that doesn't invigorate and excite you is just plain foolish, and you've got no one to point the finger of blame at but yourself. You are in control, and you must be the one to push the eject button if your present lot in life isn't turning you on.

Every professional step you take from an early age should be leading you towards your ultimate goals. Understand and accept that there will be sidesteps, detours, and obstacles along the way, but to be successful you can never lose sight of your destination. I honestly believe this is as easily done as said because loving what you do boils down to doing what you love. How you earn a living doesn't qualify as work if the excitement of the coming day keeps you awake at night. I don't *have* to get out there and swim with the sharks in the entertainment industry's swimming pool; I *get* to. Interviewing celebrities, awarding game show contestants cash and prizes, inspiring people from all walks of life to exceed their own expectations from the speaking stage, and hosting live events is not what I do, *it is who I am.*

At the young age of thirteen, I recognized the incredible talents of the local radio disc jockeys in my hometown of St. Louis. They added so much flair to my listening experience. Back then, we were exposed to "personalities" rather than the syndicated voices we hear today. These jocks are often broadcasting from thousands of miles of away rather than locally and are restricted to offering little more than scripted promos and Wikipedia stats.

On television, it was Johnny Carson who first made me take notice of the fact that one did not need to be an actor or a comedian to entertain millions of people. I reserve the right to speak often of Johnny and shall, from time to time, come back to the influence he had on me. People loved him for the man they viewed on TV and the man they suspected he was off the air. Every guy wanted to have a beer with Johnny Carson, and every woman wanted to sleep with him.

Bob Barker became just as much of a staple of daytime programming as Johnny was at night. After taking over the reins of *The Price Is Right* in 1972, Bob went on to become a household name that was synonymous with sick days from school and soap operas. For thirty-five years, Bob made the show about much more than just the games by naturally inspiring laughs and acquiring countless kisses on the cheek from ladies young and not-so-young. He made it look effortless. The moments just presented themselves. As Mr. Barker would later teach me in many private conversations, each contestant has a backstory. Each person is on that stage for a reason. The real talent lies in finding out what those stories and reasons are and sharing them with the audience at home. He could very easily have introduced viewers to Helen from Butte, MT, and gone right on to play Plinko, but instead we met "Helen, a grandmother of twelve who traveled over a thousand miles to get here, and she wants to win a vacation. It would be the first time she's left the great state of Montana since she retired fifteen years ago. Helen, let's play!" He didn't recite a line; he painted a picture that we, his loyal friends and true, were a part of.

Therein lies the difference between a run-of-the-mill emcee and a host that America cannot get enough of. The fancy suits and overpriced hair products are just window dressing for the passion that must be present to succeed in the cut-throat, rejection-laden streets of Hollywood. Lest this sound simple, let me assure you that being adoringly cheesy isn't at all easy. In fact, it is often the most difficult thing in the world to be.

The Host with the Most, named for the moniker I trademarked in 2015, is an autobiographical extension of my first book, *Life In The Bonus Round: A Game Show Host's Road To Success and Fulfillment*. I am very proud of that book as it was named Best Autobiography at the prestigious Beverly Hills Book Awards and the proceeds of its sales continue to benefit thousands of children and their families through my charity, Newton Fund 4 Kids.

Most of all, I am proud of the fact that the book shines a light on a pathway to happiness that anyone can follow at any stage of life. My life is perfectly balanced and divided into two categories, both of which I hold dear. My family life is far and away what is most sacred to me. I cherish every moment with my children and would pay a king's ransom for the ability to stop time, but that is not meant to be. So, as an alternative, I strive to make every minute count when we are together. My experiences as a father have made me a better man. They have tested my strength, schooled me in the art of being patient, and exposed me to an entirely new meaning of joy. It is during these precious moments at home that I am truly at peace.

My professional life is also treasured. With no disrespect intended, I cannot imagine trading even one year of this career for a 9 to 5 desk job. As of this writing, I have logged more than two million airline miles and achieved Platinum status with nearly every hotel and car rental rewards program. I've eaten the best and the worst food this world has to offer. My love life has taken a distant back seat to my profession, and I have not had a night out with the boys since the early nineties, but I am programmed to do nothing else but host. I don't want it; I need it. That is why I have never called in sick, never missed a flight, and never turned in a second-rate performance.

For the most part, I am self-taught. There is no substitute for throwing one's self into a pot of stew and stirring it up until you become the desired main course. That is what my friend and former MTV VJ Asher Benrubi meant when he preached his "University of Doin' It" philosophy. The most important professional lessons have been revealed over time, through falling, and through the generous mentoring of those who have been there before me. The importance of integrity and hustle, honesty and drive, and a sheer resiliency to what many refer to as rejection have all been the bullets in my gun that keep me relevant in the ever-evolving world of show business. Where I was once seen and treated (and paid) as the rookie, I am now enjoying a degree of respect and reverence that one receives when he or she is looked at as having been to the dance once or twice before. I've lived high-on-the-hog, but I've also had to watch my nickels, and I know which one makes me a happier man. I want to *be* the best so that I can *enjoy* the best. And while that includes certain luxuries, it also means having the means to be of service to others. We're all on this spinning rock together, so we need to spread love, have a few laughs, and kick a little ass while the ride is in motion.

Everyone has his/her own unique story. Some are unquestionably more captivating than others, and certain individuals have a knack for weaving a good tale, but there is no substitute for experience. Nothing is more convincing or compelling than hearing a story told straight from the horse's mouth. I admit to being someone who has been there and most likely done it. And the things I haven't done have probably been passed on by choice.

In these pages, you will join me in front of the camera, behind the microphone, and on the road as I openly share my own tales. These are some of the paths I've taken that are normally reserved for a group of close friends over a cold vodka with a splash of pineapple juice. There are some adventures that only those who were there will ever know of and others that I will relay only to my children in hopes of guiding them as they collect experiences of their own. You'll discover that I am not weighed down with regret nor am I a believer in looking back. There is always something to scoop up and take with you regardless of the pain or the frustration you may need to sift through; a skill consistently found in people who have beaten the odds in order to live the dream... *their* dream.

In the *New York Times* Bestseller, *Think Like a Champion*, Donald Trump writes, "Life is a performance art." Love him or hate him, it is important to understand that as a performer, you have a responsibility to your audience to perform to the best of your ability." The goal of my book is not merely to entertain you: that seems trite, and you deserve much more than that. Instead, I have set out to interest you with words of truth, honesty, and what I call the A.W.E. Effect: with *Age* comes *Wisdom* through *Experience*. My hope is that once I've succeeded in that performance, everything else will fall into place. If you laugh and feel inspired along the way then all the better. *The Host With The Most* is the textbook for the "University of Doin' It."

Todd Newton
St. John's, Newfoundland, Canada

CHAPTER 1

A FIFTH GRADE NIGHTMARE

"**M**R. NEWTON, SIT down and shut up... *right now!*"
Mr. Shinskey was trembling with rage. The laughter that rolled through the classroom just moments before had now completely subsided. His pudgy, mustached face, trained solely on me, was flushed with the frustration that could only come from the antics of an ill-behaved eleven-year-old boy with a knack for being the center of attention.

His chest was heaving rhythmically underneath the confines of a snug, short-sleeved button-down shirt as he struggled to control his breathing. A stray wisp of hair, which he habitually finger-combed over to the left side of his otherwise bald head, had joined me in disobedience and now flailed wildly over his eye. His rapid heart rate was further evident by the throbbing, steady beating of his left temple. Had the school nurse happen to have wandered by our classroom and peeked inside, she would have insisted that Mr. Shinskey lie down posthaste.

My fifth-grade teacher had every cause to be irate with me. He, like so many of our educators, was overworked and underpaid. No doubt he'd spent a portion of the previous evening's leisure time constructing the lesson he was now attempting to deliver to this classroom of young minds. I however, saw my schoolmates in a different light. To me, the boys and girls seated stoically at their desks were not future parents or the leaders of tomorrow. They were not flowers ready to sprout from the fertile soil of learning. In my eyes, they were something much grander.

To me, they were an audience.

My desk was in the back of the classroom near an open window. I always chose that location when given the freedom to do so. From that angle, I had an unobstructed view of the entire room. Though not as clearly as if I were wearing my prescribed eyeglasses, if the lighting was just right, I may have even been able to actually read the lessons being written on the chalkboard.

The warm temperatures teased of the summer vacation looming just a few weeks away. The allure of the green fields and fresh air outside the window to my left was too great of a temptation to ignore. I needed to stretch. To find some sort of escape from the academic monotony.

With Mr. Shinskey's teachings failing to hold my attention, I took to constructing a paper airplane. It was an elaborate design for a fifth grader. Taking a break from the more popular streamlined paper planes of the day, the chosen compact square build almost ensured a long and slow flight down from the third story classroom. All I needed was an opportunity for takeoff to present itself.

"Do it," mouthed my friend John Goodson from the desk next to mine. "He's not looking."

At such a young age, I had only recently discovered the allure of generating laughter from those around me. I had begun to recognize that unmistakable sparkle in a person's eye that comes from being genuinely entertained and found it romantic on a level that I was too inexperienced to define. For no other reason but my own vanity, it served as an energy source that I grew to need over time. And that need is what set my little plane free.

Down and down it drifted as the crisp notebook paper held dearly on to the tiny air pockets. Paper airplanes were second only to video games in my day and the singsong descent caused every one of my classmates to sit up and peer out of the window. Unfortunately for me, the show was soon over as Shinskey's attention too, had been directed outdoors.

Sensing a need to regain some semblance of control and authority, the veteran educator thought it wise to make an example of young Todd Newton.

"Todd, " he began calmly. "I want you to get up, go down, and pick that up. *Now!*"

I may have been the class clown, but I was not disobedient. I was the one who threw the plane out of the window, and I should be the one to retrieve it. But, unbeknownst to me, as I was making my way outside, Shinskey instructed each of the other students to remove a piece of paper from their Trapper Keepers, wad it up, and throw it out of the window. When I rounded the corner to collect my single piece of garbage, I was met with thirty paper balls strewn across the yard of the school.

Today I can appreciate the humor in such a stunt if it had been done in jest, but that was done out of anger. The teacher had involved the other children in his act of retribution, and it didn't sit right with me. I believed back then, as I do today, that we are responsible for ourselves. But there is a great divide between being the clown and playing the fool. The mess before me was Mr. Shinskey's doing. Not mine.

My little aeronautic masterpiece had survived the flight without as much as a wrinkle. I proudly picked it up and paraded back up to the classroom, leaving the remaining litter where it sat. The difference between right and wrong is always evident. Sometimes we just need to look past the screaming fifth-grade teacher to see it clearly.

There is a musical number called "Husky Boy" in my upcoming one-man play, *The Adventures of the Most Amazing Man on the Planet*, which makes light of my struggle with weight as a young boy. It wasn't necessarily a battle, and it didn't create any emotional scars that I've carried with me into adulthood, but being a chubby kid can definitely be tough. I ate too much and exercised too little until I realized that I could take control and turn things around. But during those hefty adolescent years, I found that giving rise to laughter among my friends was a nice tool to have when most of the girls were drawn to the more sleek physique.

Each day, I found myself looking for opportunities to engage the young ladies in tall tales and would relish in the captivated silence of those listening as they hungrily absorbed detail after animated detail. These fables, often told under a large tree hovering over the rear corner of Wohlwend Elementary School's playground, would feature all the jokes, impersonations, and embellishments my young mind could foster. It would not qualify as standup comedy. It wasn't anything resembling acting. It was the better parts of both and then some. A one-kid play, if you will. And the girls ate it up.

Around the age of thirteen was when I first witnessed Johnny Carson on television. Every kid knew of Johnny as being the guy our parents stayed awake at night to watch. I can recall lying in my bed, tucked away snugly in my St. Louis Cardinals sheets, listening to the sound of my father from our living room laughing at that night's monologue. Since taking over as host of *The Tonight Show* after the great Jack Parr in 1962, Johnny put millions of Americans to bed each weeknight until his graceful retirement thirty years later. Three decades of topical insight, informal interviews, and the occasional comedy sketch that never failed to end the viewer's day on a high note and send them off to sleep with a smile. A greater gift no entertainer can possibly offer.

Somewhere in my young mind, Johnny's appeal struck a chord. Perhaps it was hearing my beloved grandmother, Nana, repeat something he'd said the night before or hearing Dad's unmistakable chuckle as I lie in the darkness, I knew Johnny had a unique way of connecting to everyone regardless of age, sex, or geographic location. And he did it without needing to pretend to be something he was not. Though he attended many Academy Awards, he did so as Master of Ceremonies. Though he often headlined in Las Vegas, his appearances could hardly be categorized as shtick or slapstick. America fell in love with Johnny for simply being

Johnny. He was charming, self-deprecating, and fully engaged in every conversation he took part in, whether it be with Frank Sinatra or a twelve-year-old girl who could play "Chopsticks" with her toes. Mr. Carson was, and always will be, the quintessential host.

Once I was mature enough to become more suitably equipped to interpret Johnny's skill set, I began drawing comparisons between it and the reactions my schoolyard antics were generating. Thus, the seeds of my future were planted in the fertile soil of my youth.

The term *host* had yet to be officially introduced to me, but conceptually, I was completely taken by it. I began to see other personalities on television who were info-taining millions via their own voices. From news anchors to satirists, I started to formulate my dream. It was communication and camaraderie rolled into one. The light that was burning inside of me would only grow brighter and become hotter as the years passed and I became exposed to more of what the world of show business had to offer.

My first recollection of professional ambition was a deep longing to become a radio disc jockey. Like most kids of my generation and generations before, it was the high-energy, personality driven rock 'n roll DJ's of the day that added so much to the experience of turning the radio on and getting lost in the theater of the mind.

On its own, music has a distinct way of taking us to places we have never been and arousing emotions that we have never felt. Much like many of the tattoos on my body, my favorite songs remind me of people and times in my life that make me feel safe and warm. And feeling *good* is really what life is all about. I love feeling good. When we're sad, we want to be happy. When we miss someone, we want to be with them again. Music has the power to change our emotional state in just a few bars. But, as previously touched upon, for me it was what I heard between those records that made listening to the radio an event rather than simply a way to pass the time. The music made me feel the way I wanted to feel, but the voices coming from my stereo would change my life.

Night after night, I would lie on my bedroom floor with my head positioned as close to the speakers as possible. The voices of Chris Knight, "Big Ron" O' Brien and my favorite, Jimmy Paige "The Nighttime Rage" would tickle my inner ear with a dance of bass, speed, and inflection. In the mid 1980's, St. Louis was a radio market to be reckoned with and the level of talent one heard on the airwaves was a clear demonstration of the city's value to the music industry. Many have said that caliber of on air performance would not be heard again until almost a decade later.

While most of the on air personalities possessed the required booming chops and the savoir-faire listeners were craving, Jimmy Paige took it to a whole new stratosphere. Paige hosted the 7pm-midnight show on the Gateway City's leading Top 40 radio station, WKBQ. Unbeknownst to me at the time, this was the very same time slot that I would come to own years later. Jimmy was the first jock I remember listening to who had mastered the art of "hitting the post"-a term referring to speaking right up until the first word or a significant musical note of the song. His talk breaks always consisted of rhymes, callers off of the request lines, and even the occasional sound effect. The amount of effort and care he showed when he opened the microphone was evident and to this day is mostly unparalleled.

As fate would have it, Jimmy and I found ourselves working together in the early nineties at KHTK HOT 97. Sadly, the industry had beaten him down by then and his on air performance wasn't nearly as dynamic as it once had been. However, I had just jumped off the starting line of my career and, as I've done so many times over the years, recognized an opportunity to better myself by studying him.

Much like Bob Barker would do in years to come, Jimmy allowed me to sit quietly in the back of the studio and observe him in his natural habitat. Barely did I blink as I watched his fingers play the control board like a church organ. Not only did he never miss a beat, he somehow seemed to create beats that weren't there before and incorporate them into his delivery. As the music played, he'd be busy organizing his next bit and speaking to listeners on the phone. Many radio personalities use the request lines as their private dating service, but Jimmy was different. In addition to using pauses and colorful adjectives to paint beautiful word pictures, I learned from JP to see the request line as my own personal focus group. Later I would utilize it as a source of direct contact with those who would allow me to continue to create. To me the audience has always been the real test. Ratings and demographics are an important part of the business, but the listeners are the ones who have kept the lights on and food on the table. Speaking to the audience one at a time, whether on the phone, by email, or through social media, has given me the ability to hear exactly what they want and then deliver it to them on a silver platter. Jimmy Paige was adamant that the listener always come before the business.

Tragedy struck not long into my unofficial apprenticeship when Jimmy Paige lost his life in a horrific boating accident. The St. Louis radio audience was stunned. We had lost a star. One night this larger than life personality was there on our radios, the next night he was gone. It was shocking and his passing left a void in FM radio that has never been filled. Fortunately, months before, he had presented me with a cassette tape of what he believed to be some of his finest work. I believe it was his way of passing the baton and encouraging me to keep his animated and interactive style of on air delivery alive. The plastic and ribbon components of the tape have worn and faded due to the passing of time but upon careful listening, it is still ninety minutes of what radio should be: a medium designed to allow the listener to escape reality for a little while and feel *good*.

A mutual friend of ours, Steve Byes, is another St. Louis radio legend who was probably closer to Jimmy than anyone. When I announced that I was leaving the local airwaves in 1995 to work for E! in Los Angeles, Stevie B. bid me farewell by presenting me with Paige's production reel consisting of his personal collection of favorite bits, commercials, and highlights. It meant the world to me then and means even more to me now.

I rediscovered the Paige tapes during my move from Los Angeles to Boston and immediately sent the entire collection to a company in Nashville to have them converted to digital format. It wasn't a day too soon either as time and the salty effects of living by the ocean had begun to take a toll on my delicate collection. Now, when I find myself scrolling through those files on my iPad while traveling, I'll occasionally click on one of Jimmy's old riffs and make a mental note to share it with my own radio audience.

"I'm playin' the biggest hitties in the city and one hour commercial free, bay-beee!"

"This is Todd Newton standin' tall against the wall with hits up to my pits!"

Old school radio should never have gone out of style, regardless of what corporate America dictates. A great disc jockey is like a pair of worn-in Levis jeans or your favorite Chuck Taylor Converse sneakers. They are classics that were here fifty years ago, and they'll still make you feel just as good fifty years down the road. When you sacrifice personality in order to stuff in an extra mattress store commercial, you are pulling beautiful feathers from the peacock's behind. Keep plucking away and you will soon be left with nothing but an ugly, naked bird shivering in shame.

Prior to becoming the rookie on the KHTK air staff, I first cracked the St. Louis airwaves at a small college radio station called 88.9 KYMC. It was there in a broom closet-sized studio tucked away in the campus library that I learned another lesson that I'd carry with me throughout my career: the majority of people you'll encounter throughout your life are just downright lazy. There's no other way to put it. Most individuals expect success to come and find them, but for whatever reason they fail to put in the work that is required. There is a false sense of entitlement in this country that is detrimental to the development of future generations. I'll tell you what I always tell my children: If you want the secret to happiness, here it is...*work your ass off for it*!

When you've set your sights on success, you must be willing to laugh at phrases like "above and beyond" and "no pain, no gain." That type of thinking is what I call "bumper sticker logic." It alludes to the existence of boundaries and limitations and it won't lead you anywhere. Instead you have to train your mind, body, and soul to accept discomfort and embrace the unimaginable. Flexibility will need to be your new best friend. Sacrifice and rejection will soon be your co-pilots, and you'll need to be okay with that. In fact, you'll have to invite sacrifice and rejection in.

When I discovered that KYMC didn't broadcast between 1 a.m. and 3 a.m. each day simply because no one wanted to get out of bed to do a show, I took the shift. No radio station was going to sit silently on my watch. I wanted to be a radio star too badly. When calls from record labels came in I picked up the phone and began establishing contacts. When high schools reached out to the station looking to book a disc jockey for the homecoming dance, I showed up free of charge to build my listenership. The more others sat around drinking coffee and complaining about the weather, the faster my career grew.

KYMC was just over twenty miles away from my parents' home and the 1986 Cutlass Supreme I drove at the time had certainly seen better days. When people tell me that money can't buy happiness, I always respond by telling them it really depends on what makes you happy. Personally, knowing that my kids are eating nutritious food, having access to good healthcare, and owning a car that I am confident will start each time I put the key in the ignition are three things that make me extremely happy. And all three of those things cost money.

My car was in rough shape. Normally I would need to stop at the all-night gas station to add a healthy dose antifreeze or power steering fluid just to ensure that I'd be able make it all the way to the station. This not only added time to each leg of the journey, but expense, as well. But the payoff was worth the investment and I accepted the added charges as the cost of doing business. Being me isn't free. The same goes for you.

The real adventure began when I would finally arrive at the campus studio. Since I was working such obscene hours, the library that housed the radio station would be locked up tight and I'd have to track down the overnight janitor on foot to let me in. This could be torturous during the cold St. Louis winter months and, admittedly, there were those rare occasions where I wondered if it was worth the headache. But as soon as he opened the door and the red on air light came on everything seemed right with the world. We were barely audible outside of the campus boundaries, but I was officially on the radio and that was all that mattered.

My young body soon adjusted to the nocturnal schedule and I was able to work that to my advantage when I applied for a position at a commercial radio station closer to home. Being awake while others slept meant that I had doubled the number of productive hours I had in a day. I would often leave KYMC and drive straight to what I felt was my ticket to the Big Show, an unpaid internship at KHKT. Because I was eager to take on the work that others were not-to feed on the table scraps-I was afforded the opportunity to learn the radio business through trial and error. Falling on my face and finding out what didn't work became my curriculum. Failure is the greatest of all teachers because it is honest and raw. Like the Swedish script tattoo on my wrist reads:

Lyckan star den djarve bi.

Translation: Fortune favors the bold.

Once I began to find my own voice my life started to change. Even though I was operating on the lowest rung of the ladder and missing the immediate gratification of my friends' laughter, there was no denying that my dream was now in motion. I was eighteen and unstoppable. I could see, hear, and feel the beginning of an on air persona cracking through the surface. Like a baby bird hatching from the egg, I was in a constant state of discovery. Each listener that called the request line represented acceptance from the audience. There were a million things that a man or woman (usually a woman) could be doing with their time but they were calling me.

When I'd receive honest feedback from a professional in the field, whether it be constructive or positive, my hunger to reach for the golden ring would only intensify. With each air shift the vision I had for myself became clearer and more detailed as if coming into focus through the lens of a camera. With each passing day I became more and more determined to become the greatest radio personality of my generation. The fire that burns just as hot inside of me today as it did in Mr. Shinskey's fifth-grade classroom is the foundation for everything that I have and everything that I want. Without that drive and the freedom to pursue it, I don't know what I may have become.

Like most parents who will read this book, I have on one or two occasions met with my children's teachers to discuss their academic progress. Now and again the issue of behavior will come up and it never fails to bring a grin to my face when I am told that one or both of my kids has a tendency to "act up" or "strive to be the center of attention." I then explain that we will be happy to discuss boundaries with the kids, but will not under any circumstances do or say anything to squash their love for that kind of feedback. Not only because being the class clown happens to be how Dad makes a living, but because lucky is the child who discovers something that fuels them at such a young age. Passion is not taught in school. Neither is persistence, persuasion, or courage. It deserves to be encouraged and supported, not reprimanded.

Uncovering a desire that will be with you for an entire lifetime is one of life's greatest rewards.

CHAPTER 2

AND HERE'S YOUR HOST

I AM A DREAMER of the tallest order. But I cannot say that I dream in the traditional sense. I don't close my eyes and have visions of unicorns frolicking through marshmallow-covered pastures while I sleep. Instead, I have come to accept that what occurs during slumber can better be categorized as thinking. I've also discerned over time that these thoughts are not only logical, but have also proven to be beneficial. While my body relishes in necessary rest and the batteries recharge, my mind focuses on conversations I was a part of, examines decisions that need to be made, or itemizes the tasks for the next day. I've read accounts of other people throughout history that have claimed to have experienced the same phenomenon. Perhaps it gives me a bit of an edge or maybe I am really missing out on the whole dream thing, but either way, it has become a part of my process.

It should then come as no surprise that I rarely have a problem jumping out of bed in the morning. I am ready to go before my alarm even sounds and, aided by the occasional power nap, feel fully productive throughout the day. It is not unusual for me to host an event in Las Vegas that lasts until midnight, return to my hotel room for a few hours of sleep, and be one of the first to arrive at the airport to catch the 6 am flight to New York only to walk onto another stage and deliver my *The Choice Is Yours* keynote speech to a corporation that evening. I have always been a last-flight-in-first-flight-out type of business traveler, thus maximizing every hour of every day and allowing me to maintain the hustle while enjoying as much time at home with my family as possible. Not to say that have any more time in my day than you have in yours, I just may use what I have a little more strategically because the artistic challenge of my work provides the fuel to do so. Anyone who enjoys a high level of success in their field will tell you that they believe in working while the competition is sleeping. Train your mind and body to sleep on planes, boats, or in the backseat of any car so you can be ready and able to jump to attention when the moment presents itself. They say the struggle is real, but what they never tell you is that the reward is always worth it.

Rarely will I turn down the opportunity to work. I put too much energy into my career to say "No thank you," simply because I am tired. I love the money. I love the satisfaction that comes from providing for my family. I love the exposure. I love the experience. I love falling into bed at night exhausted from a solid day's work. It goes against everything I believe in to allow someone else to step in and fill the role just because of fatigue. Greedy? Maybe. Ambitious? Without question. Investing time is the drug of choice to a workaholic.

I was sound asleep in my bunk when our giant, midnight black tour bus pulled up outside the 3,000 seat theater in northern California. It had been less than eight hours since I'd reminded the previous night's audience of approximately the same size to have their pets spayed and neutered, and tonight I would have the privilege of delivering one of the most recognized lines in television history once again.

As the customized Prevost hissed to a stop, I rolled out from the rear middle sleeping compartment on the passenger's side and felt my way through the darkness, blindly searching for the button that would silently slide open the door that separates bunk alley from the front lobby area. Someone, most likely our tour manager whom we affectionately refer to as Mama Bear, had put a pot of coffee on. The glorious aroma set the tone for another day on the road. I filled the ceramic mug that my daughter and I made together before the launch of the tour which serves as my good luck charm when I travel, collected my bags, and stiffly descended the three steps to the parking lot to fill my lungs with fresh morning air.

Life on a tour bus is not for everyone, but I have taken to it quite nicely. With the demanding schedule we keep, often a different city each night for weeks on end, traveling by commercial airline would be inconceivable on many levels. The twelve-passenger bus allows us to cover hundreds of miles a night while maintaining a routine of regular sleep, dining, and exercise that keeps the crew sharp. Plus, I find it rather adventurous exploring North America with my fellow game show gypsies. The buses we travel in for the live game show are state-of-the-art; equipped with everything from Wi-Fi and satellite TV to full kitchen facilities. These babies give a whole new meaning to "road tripping" and the opportunity to see this great country of ours from the highway is something everyone should experience.

As much I cherish relaxing in the plush leather seats and binge watching my favorite shows while cruising at seventy miles per hour, nothing compares to the excitement of finally reaching our destination. It's the grown-up version of *are we there yet?* Performing is all many of us know how to do and when you first see the venue growing larger and larger through the windshield you can't help but be reminded that you are getting paid to live the dream.

Because no two audiences are the same, no two shows can ever be the same. The only thing one can expect with each new performance is the *un*expected. For a variety of economic, religious, and societal reasons, folks are different all over the country. What may have gone over extremely well at the Saenger Theater in Mobile, Alabama, may fall flat with the folks at the Stanley Theater in Utica, New York. Our crowds include the young and the old. Generations of families attend together because of what *The Price Is Right* has meant to them over the years.

From the stage I often recognize groups of co-workers looking to bond outside of the workplace. It's also easy to pick out those young couples who have chosen our show as their first date. At one performance in Indiana we even had a woman in the audience who brought her pet macaque monkey to the theater because he enjoyed sitting on her shoulder while she watched the show at home on television. It came as a shock to me that this breed of animal views the flashing of teeth as a sign of aggression, so when I smiled my big game show host smile and tried to pet him, he hissed and assumed a battle position. It was a terrifying, primal sight and I was honestly startled! But in traditional host fashion, I quickly reacted as any seasoned professional would: I put the microphone up to my mouth and declaring, "You could win thiiiiiis!" Nothing lightens the mood like the chance to win a new refrigerator.

In any business one must be able to adapt to the ever-changing needs and wants of our customers. This constant evolution and the demand to remain relevant keeps me on my show business toes and (I'd like to think) at the top of my game. Call it built-in incentive. When you respect the fact that people are paying their hard-earned money to see you do your thing, you better make sure your thing is worth seeing.

Hosting a live game show is different from other projects because it comes with the challenge of never knowing who may be joining you on stage as a contestant. Many people have approached me in restaurants after a show and asked, "Was that all real? Be honest, some of that was staged, right?" That's an enormous compliment because it shows that what we did that night was so good the audience assumed it must have been pre-arranged. The answer, of course, is nothing we do is staged. If I wanted to be in a play I would study acting. There are no ringers or scripts to be followed in hosting and no second takes if the first wasn't perfect. If what you saw seemed slick and seamless, it's only appeared that way because the people who were doing it are the best. Thousands of shows under our belts indicate that our passion translates into a performance people enjoy.

But as is the case with any live production, the audience plays a vital role in the show's success.

The same is true when I deliver my *The Choice Is Yours* presentation to a corporation or university. Though the crowds may be a bit smaller in size, the talk is extremely interactive. *Choice* was designed to allow me the flexibility of incorporating crowd work into it. In any given sixty minute talk, I may spend a total of thirty-five minutes on the actual stage. The rest of the time I am maneuvering through rows of seats, strolling up and down the aisles, and have even been known to stand on a chair or two. The finished product may appear easy and glamorous because we all have smiles on our faces, but it is work. It's a job that requires countless hours of writing, scheduling, and rehearsals that the audience never sees or even considers. The time on stage is the easy part. It's the other twenty-three hours in the day that can wear you down. But when you love what you do it always shines through in the finished product.

The same spontaneity that often arises in game shows can also appear when conducting an interview. The man or woman holding the microphone must always be prepared to stay in control of the conversation no matter where it may the interviewee may lead it. Some of my favorite celebrities to interview during my twelve years at E! Entertainment Television were those stars who were unpredictable in their responses.

The first time I met the late, great Robin Williams was in 1993 at a private function for Disney. Robin was riding a massive wave of success stemming from the *Aladdin* animated films and my cameraman, Harold Henderson, and I were lucky to get to speak to him just as he arrived. He was always friendly in a fatherly sort of way. Harold was positioning us just right and making sure we were in focus while Robin just stared at me with that tight-lipped grin that was his signature look. From the moment the camera began rolling, I was dumbfounded by the speed at which Robin's mind worked. The questions I asked made no difference. Robin was going to take me where he wanted to take me and the most I could do was hang on and enjoy the wild ride. Many of my entertainment news colleagues suspect that Robin always knew what he was going to say and that was how he was able to be as frantic and off-the-cuff as he was. I don't believe that to be true. The words spewing from Robin's lips were merely letters or sound particles accumulating in his brain just milliseconds before. The two of us eventually found a nice groove and our conversations always came across as chummy on the air. I can't say with any certainty if Robin Williams ever watched any of our interviews on television, but over the course of the next ten years he always accommodated my requests to speak and would often throw those hairy arms around me and refer to me as "Toddy, my boy."

John Ritter was arguably one of the most impressive improvisational comedians of the past fifty years. Known primarily for his Emmy and Golden Globe winning role as Jack Tripper on the hit sitcom *Three's Company*, John is revered as having impeccable comedic timing and for being a master of the prop fall. The legendary Don Knotts even referred to Ritter as "the greatest physical comedian on the planet."

Shortly before his death in 2003, I had the opportunity to co-host the Creative Arts Emmy Awards with John at the Beverly Hilton Hotel in Beverly Hills, CA. Prior to the ceremony, we were introduced to one another backstage. During our brief conversation, I attempted to connect with him by mentioning that I had studied improv at the Harvey Lembeck Comedy Workshop, as I knew he had. John's eyes lit up as he spoke of his years training at the academy. It was clearly a special and formative time in his career. In addition to John and myself, past Lembeck students include Sharon Stone, Kim Cattrall, Scott Baio, and even Robin Williams.

Developing my improv skills under the guidance of the brother/sister coaching team of Helaine and Michael Lembeck, and later at The Groundlings, became an invaluable resource in my hosting aresenal. My years of sharing those tiny, dimly lit stages with fellow performers taught me how to maximize a moment, capitalize on a pause, and prepare for any possible outcome of a scene. I was able to workshop ideas in a judgment-free environment, and that form of fearless training has prevented me from ever being caught off guard on camera.

That night in Beverly Hills was unique as I would be sharing the stage with not only a professional but a master. Always the entertainer, John immediately began searching for ways the two of us could make our time on stage something memorable for the audience. He realized, as did I, that the black tie crowd was only there for the awards and the open bar. It usually takes no more than fifteen minutes for their attention span to lapse. Such a stiff atmosphere often makes for a tough outing as a presenter.

Here I was backstage with a comedy legend batting ideas around like a couple of kittens with a ball of yarn. John would throw something out there and ask what I thought. I'd make suggestions and he'd listen intently. He made me feel like an equal even though I was barely qualified to stand in his shadow. I'm not sure anyone could have gone toe-to-toe with him in the comedy ring, but I found this brainstorming session exhilarating. Comedy is rarely as spontaneous as it appears and when more than one performer is involved the complexity of the choreography rivals that of a ballet. By watching him work, I experienced a real a-ha moment: it's the risk of failing that makes the successes so jubilant. I have rarely enjoyed the creative process as much as I did that night on Wilshire Boulevard with John Ritter.

Finally, he hit upon a concept that I agreed would have the audience reaching for their overpriced handkerchiefs to wipe away the tears of laughter.

"Every time you begin to read off of the teleprompter I'll step on you as if our lines got crossed. You be the straight man and just continue on and I'll play the stooge," he said. "The better you read, the dumber I'll look. Let's just see where it takes us." Again, there was no concern about the risk of John looking ridiculous because if it paid off it would be the funniest segment of the night. I had complete confidence in him and in myself. Together we were going to go for broke.

Sure enough, John's instincts were spot on. The two of us made our way to the stage and as the introduction music faded, I proceeded to read my lines off of the giant teleprompter positioned at the back of the ballroom. John immediately turned and began responding to me as if he thought my lines were intended for him. I gave him a look as if I was put out by the intrusion and he lobbed the moment back to me by apologizing profusely.

Again and again, I would attempt to move to the next category of awards and each time he would masterfully cut in. John appeared to become increasingly confused. The more he nervously ran his fingers through his hair in complete humiliation the more the crowd ate it up. Though my eyes were focused on the large screen and my next line, I could see and feel John fidgeting to my right. He was so convincing in this setup that I could sense genuine desperation radiating from him. He was in complete control of a situation that appeared to be spiraling downward in a hurry. We were oil and water. A minor league Martin and Lewis. It was a beautiful chaos masterminded by a genius. And though he was clearly the star, the moment was both of ours to share.

John Ritter could have easily outshone me that night. He could have made me disappear in the eyes of an audience filled with Hollywood heavyweights. But he didn't. Quite the opposite. Not only did he give me a memory I will never forget, John Ritter made me a better host.

Jim Carrey and Dana Carvey also forced me to pay closer attention to the moment and proved to be valid tests of my professional patience. Both men had the ability to transform themselves into other people before my very eyes, thus making it difficult to get a solid soundbite I could use for a television broadcast. E! was very liberal and tolerant in the early days, but no network likes sending a crew to an event only to have nothing to air the next day.

With Dana, I routinely took the approach of having a few questions in mind that I would use should he slip into the character of President Bush or Garth from *Wayne's World*. I found it was in these different personas where he seemed the most comfortable and where I'd get the best interview. This strategy worked extremely well at a charity tennis tournament in Malibu. Not thirty seconds into our conversation, the Church Lady from Dana's *SNL* days suddenly appeared and we were off to races. What his publicist said would be a three minute interview ended up being five times that because he was allowed to operate from a place of artistic freedom. He wasn't being required to be or say anything in particular. It was completely up to the Church Lady. When the camera went off he returned to being himself. Spending time with Dana was a unique and welcomed challenge during that phase of my career.

Giving up the punch line and letting the guest have the laugh is one of the greatest challenges for many hosts who are currently occupying high profile positions. Johnny mastered the ability to do just that, to take a backseat to the guest. Jay Leno did not. Meaning no disrespect, Jay was trained in comedy clubs then thrown into the most revered chair on television. A tiger never changes his stripes. The same can be said for many of today's late-night talk show hosts who come from the world of stand up. What should be a conversation often feels more like a routine one might see at an open mic night on the Sunset Strip. When I am wearing my hosting mask I focus on letting the guest or the contestant have the shining moment.

During a performance in Glenside, PA, a woman named Linda joined me on stage to play a game for a significant amount of money. During our brief back and forth exchange, she told me that she and her husband were celebrating their twenty-fifth anniversary that night. What an honor for our show that the two of them chose to share such a milestone event in their lives with us.

I felt as if the audience may like to know more about the two of them so I dove into my bag of questions and pulled out a couple of my favorites. I must state for the record that "Yes or No" questions can be the death of a great moment on stage or on camera. One word answers leave you with nothing to work with and nowhere to go. If you ask a great open-ended question and still get a single syllable response it can be funny and natural. But if you ask, "Are you having fun tonight?" and they respond with a simple "Yes," it will more than likely become so silent in the room that you'll be able to hear the ticking of your own watch. The questions I choose to ask, whether it is to an Academy Award nominee or a local lottery winner from a small town in Tennessee, demand a well-articulated answer.

"Tell me about the first time you laid eyes on that husband of yours," I said to Linda. Not a question per se, but an open door to share one of the most pivotal experiences of her life.

I saw her smile and knew the memory brought back special feelings, but I could not have predicted her response in a million lifetimes. "I met that man in federal prison!"

After taking a moment to process the unexpected comeback, the roar of laughter from the audience began in the front row and made its way all the way to the top of the balcony section. It was the line that wrote itself. I allowed the thousands in attendance to draw their own conclusions. Fortunately, I was savvy enough to know that there was no way to follow that one. Nothing I could've come up with would have matched the gift she'd just handed to us. I must admit here that she leaned into me and whispered, "We were both corrections officers," but I opted not to share it. Let the audience have this moment and let them continue to fall in love with Linda. They cheered her on to a five thousand dollar win that night.

A woman named Betty and some of her family attended a presentation of mine in Midland, TX, a few years back to celebrate her birthday. I asked Betty to join me onstage as she was an adorable older woman who reminded me of my own grandmother, Nana. Everyone loves a grandma and Betty fit the part to a tee. As I soon discovered, it was her husband who heard about the convention and brought her to see me. "He's always doing nice things for me," she said, to which the crowd responded with a nice "Awwww...."

"Well, I think true love is beautiful," I responded. "Tell me, does he have a special pet name for you? I bet he does." This is another question that I have at the ready and always produces fantastic results.

Betty's pudgy cheeks immediately took on a rose-colored hue. "Well, yes. But I don't think he'd want me to share it with another man."

I lost it on stage. Few things beat a nicely-timed innuendo delivered by a matronly granny and it's pure gold when it happens. Much like the situation I faced with Linda, I could have chosen to let sleeping dogs lie and just moved on, but my hosting instincts were telling me to swing for the fences on this one. "Betty, I simply don't think this show could go on if we don't find out what the love of your life calls you when it's just the two of you."

If it turned out to be something along the lines of "Sweetcakes" we would all think it precious and proceed with festivities. But if it was something more colorful then someone better open up the history books and grab a pen because we're about to make magic.

She hesitated for a moment longer. I could tell she was looking to him for approval, but the spotlight was blinding and she soon realized the decision was hers and hers alone.

"He's always called me KakaChubs," Betty revealed.

KakaChubs? Really? The origins of the name-not to mention the proper spelling-were left to our individual imaginations, but all of our minds were going in the same direction: south. Everyone in the audience began repeating it to themselves over and over in an effort not to forget it. They would want to post it on Facebook, Tweet about it, and text it to their friends as soon as they could power up their phones. It was another home run and, once again, it came from reality. It was an honest look into someone's life, and that's where the real comedy can always be found. Nothing synthetic. Nothing manufactured. Nothing rehearsed.

"KakaChubs" became an instant celebrity. I saw people asking for selfies with her as she exited the auditorium and social media was blowing up with hashtags about that moment for days afterward. She was a bonafide hit and it all came from allowing the moment to happen naturally. I may have put the ball on the tee but she hit it right down the fairway.

We had the good fortune of performing in Baltimore's beautiful Lyric Opera House in April of 2015. Little did we know that the very next day Charm City would turn into a virtual war zone. Riot stemming from the funeral of a young man who suffered a severe spinal cord injury while in police custody resulted in schools being closed, cars and buildings becoming engulfed in flames, and a mandatory curfew being put into place throughout the city. The news came as a shock to all of us as we watched the live footage on CNN from the safety of our tour bus.

Just twenty-fours hours prior, I was standing on stage with a woman named Brenda who was about to play a game for a fabulous prize. Before giving her a shot to make her game show dreams come true, I asked her what she did for a living. "I'm a stay-at-home mom," she said. The audience and I both showed our appreciation for all she does on a daily basis. I'm a bit of a mama's boy, myself. My mother stayed home while my brother and I were growing up and it wasn't until adulthood that I began to appreciate fully all of the hard work and the tireless sacrifice that goes along with being a domestic goddess. I have that same appreciation for my ex-wife.

"How old are your kids?" I asked. Her response is forever burned upon my brain like the lyrics to a favorite song. "I have one twenty-six-year-old and twenty-two-year-old twins." The explosion of laughter from the 2,500 in attendance almost knocked me right off the stage. No further questions, Your Honor.

Though tension was high throughout Baltimore, that night on that stage it was all love and smiles. In fact, a popular Baltimore website reviewed the show the following day and the highlight of the article was Brenda's appearance. In his own words, the writer accurately reported what I had hoped had been conveyed:

> *"When it comes to the best game show hosts in America, Newton is one of the best personalities of our generation. He's quick with the quip. He lets the contestants be the stars and makes them feel warm and cozy. He can take an ordinary life story of a guest and make it extraordinary, as was the case with stay-at-home-mom Brenda last evening."*

The finest compliment a host can receive.

Robin Williams and John Ritter bestowed upon me the gift of professional generosity. They didn't talk about it. They graciously demonstrated it. I didn't *give* Linda the federal prison line, I just gave her the opportunity to share a bit of herself with a roomful of strangers and the moment became more memorable on its own accord. I certainly had nothing to do with Betty's term of endearment, but I guarantee people were telling that story at the office the following day. Because I care enough about my performance to study the work of the greats and pay attention to what works for me and what doesn't, I discovered that two people generally give the audience more entertainment that just one. Life is more fun when you share it the way John Ritter shared with me. Thank you, gentlemen. I am forever grateful. May you both rest in peace.

As a host, I embrace the responsibility of introducing a person to an audience in a way that creates an emotional connection. "Why should I care?" is the question they are most likely asking themselves. Hosts dig and dig until we uncover a reason for them to become invested. Bob Barker would constantly remind me from the infamous WGMC (World's Greatest Master of Ceremonies) director's chair in his CBS dressing room that every contestant has a backstory; a reason they are there. "Find it," he'd say.

Lest you question the importance of establishing rapport in your own professional life, please think back to the last time you were on an airplane. Flight attendants are not the most eloquent public speakers on the planet. In fact, their messages of safety are often lost on a plane full of disgruntled passengers who don noise canceling headphones or otherwise tune them out before the first word can be spoken.

Next time you fly I invite you to take note of the lack of emotion with which your average flight attendant speaks to the cabin. The majority demonstrate little, if any, inflection while reading the connecting gate information which makes the listener feel as if there is no heart or substance behind what they are saying. The pacing is rushed and their poor implementation of the public address system's handset makes their words virtually inaudible for the few passengers who do wish to listen.

And the repetition! One would be hard pressed to hear the phrase "once again" used more often than during airline travel. "Once again, ladies and gentlemen, welcome aboard flight 1111 nonstop to Miami." We are fully aware of our destination and do not need to be reminded of it. We consciously purchased the ticket, arranged to be picked up upon arrival, and made it onto the flight. Deciding where we would go wasn't a crap shoot or a travel lottery. The redundancy we are subjected to is a classic example of the value of word economy. Why use ten words when you can convey your message in five? Just tell me what time it is. I don't need to know how to build a clock. And why must that message include the pilot sharing his flight patterns? It is unnecessary. And the incessant *uh*'s and *um*'s are enough to make me want to pull my hair plugs out... assuming I had hair plugs.

I was recently on a flight from Burbank to Phoenix where we encountered some turbulence. For those who have ever flown in to or out of Phoenix you know this is not an uncommon occurrence because of the mountain ranges. Quite often the bumps require the flight attendants to remain seated for the duration of the flight.

As a result drink service was not offered on this particular flight. Personally, I did not feel inconvenienced by this as our flight time was just over one hour from gate to gate. The flight crew felt differently was led to apologize to the cabin *five times*. One apology is to be expected. Two apologies is being overly-considerate. Anything more than three is textbook overkill. Passengers were looking at each other in disbelief. The airline's thoughtful intent was completely lost in the delivery and the all important connection with the customer was damaged.

The most beautiful aspect of game shows is the pure and simple fact that viewers and audience members find something so appealing in a total stranger that they want to invest their energy into rooting for that person's good fortune. A viewer at home will never meet the person they see playing on television yet they are cheering them on in hopes the stranger wins that new car. The woman sitting in row JJ at the Pikes Peak Center in Colorado Springs, CO, doesn't know the contestant standing next to me on stage from Adam, yet she screams at the top of her lungs when he wins a four day/three night vacation in Las Vegas. That's game show magic and you cannot buy it or create it artificially. It comes from the heart, but it occasionally needs to be awakened and stirred. Knowing when to speak and when to let the silence do the talking is paramount in maximizing the moment. This was one of my greatest takeaways from my improv training. Proper timing requires one to be fully present and in tune with what the audience wants. Give too much and they become overwhelmed and exhausted by your banter. Give too little and they drive home feeling disappointed and shortchanged.

Host only on the professional level and your career will be fleeting. Allow your abilities to connect on an emotional level and you better pack a lunch because you're going to be around for a while.

CHAPTER 3

Make the Moment Matter

Time is all we've got. The seconds that become minutes and eventually pass as years are more precious than gold because it could all end tomorrow. Everything that matters to you in your life is a result of a series of events leading up to a particular moment in time. That is why I believe that the memories we create are life's greatest souvenirs.

Winning the Daytime Emmy Award for Outstanding Game Show Host in 2012 was the result of the tireless effort I've been pouring into my career since 1986. I have vivid memories of being an ambitious young mobile disc jockey lugging milk crates filled with vinyl records into and out of wedding receptions, American Legion halls, and the smoky bars of South St. Louis. Becoming a father, the most rewarding achievement of my life, was a result of mustering up the courage to speak to Silver, ask her out on that first date to see the film *Any Given Sunday*, propose marriage, and strive to get my emotional and financial lives in order so I could be the best provider possible for my kids.

I don't believe in fate and have never put much stock in the misleading concept of luck. It is not known for certain who first delivered the quote, "The harder I work the more luck I have." Some attribute it to Thomas Jefferson, though it has never been discovered in any of his writings. Others say it, along with many other familiar phrases, was penned by the author Coleman Cox in the early 1920's. Though the source may be unclear the message could not be more on target with a life sprinkled with success. Even athletes like Tom Brady and LeBron James, both of whom seem genetically disposed to greatness in their respective sport, maximize what they have been given with intense training and discipline. Entrepreneurs like Richard Branson and Bill Gates never stop seeking knowledge about and branching out into unchartered territories. The world is moving too quickly to kick back watch the show. Successful, fulfilled individuals believe in taking full advantage of everything life has to offer. Never, ever waste even a single moment. Never convince yourself that you know *enough*.

In my award winning book, *Life In The Bonus Round: A Game Show Host's Road To Success and Fulfillment*, I write about the importance of creating and seizing opportunities for yourself. It's not enough just to recognize a chance to move up, you have to get out into the world and mix things up. Too many people from my generation are programmed to expect good fortune to be bestowed upon them. I challenge anyone to show me where it is written that we deserve the best simply for getting out of bed in the morning. That is not how life works and to believe otherwise is poisonous. Achievement is not a right. The Constitution does not guarantee us health and happiness. These are privileges bestowed upon those who seek them out through sweat and squander.

Like any industry, the entertainment business is a down-and-dirty grind for those who want to reach the top. It is a nonstop hustle that requires the thickest of skin. As a result of incorporating the A.W.E. Effect into my life (with *Age* comes *Wisdom* through *Experience*), I have not only become immune to the rejection that is par for the course in my chosen field, I have come to welcome it. Being passed on for a project underlines the areas I need to focus on in my delivery. Maybe I'm too young for this part or too old for that one. Maybe I speak to quickly or have too many tattoos. Whatever the case may be, I see every meeting as an opportunity to become a better all around talent.

Never once have I gone home and cried about not getting hired. It's just not productive and my tears are saved for moments in my life that really matter. When I was a student at Oakville High School in St. Louis, I was cut from the freshman basketball team. I didn't make the grade. That was my introduction to rejection. The first time something that I really wanted eluded me and went to someone else. I came up with a million excuses as to why I failed, but the truth is that I just wasn't good enough. While other boys my age were running, lifting weights, and eating properly in order to get in shape for the tryouts, I was messing around with my friends and watching game shows. My feet didn't move quickly enough and my jump shot was average at best. All I really had to offer the team was my aggressive defensive play and that wasn't enough to earn a spot on the roster. I had to face the hard truth that I had been out-hustled.

After realizing that most of my friends would be wearing the black and gold and I'd be watching from the stands, I crawled into the backseat of my mother's car and wept like a baby. It was pathetic and it served no purpose. Even after all of the tears were shed and my pride was completely gone I still wasn't on the team. What good did crying do? You won't win them all, but that doesn't mean you shouldn't try. The true meaning of a winner is getting back up and going back out there after being passed on. I have been in contention for two of the longest-running non-scripted shows on television but they both alluded me. I can't afford the time it would take to mourn the loss of the piles of money those shows would have dumped into my lap or wonder "why him and not me?" There is no value in that. Instead, I chose to put forth that same energy into becoming the one they cannot refuse next time. Survive and thrive by understanding it's the jobs you get that change your life and not the gigs you lost out on. Grow from the experience. Commit yourself to everything and never stop working your tail off to be the very best. One of the doors you're banging on will open up if you knock consistently and persistently.

It's been my experience that everything leads to something. This is referred to as the butterfly effect: the theory that a small change in one state can result in large differences in a later state. Can the flapping of a butterfly's wings result in a hurricane down the line? Impossible to know. But I have seen the seeds I've planted in my life grow with wonderful results. Being kind and respectful to someone during a complex contract negotiation. Demonstrating patience during a long television taping that results in a reputation of being easy to work with. Both are examples of setting yourself up for exciting and profitable opportunities in the future.

The other side of that coin also holds true. A hot temper and a loud mouth can slam the brakes on a flourishing career. The squeaky wheel does not always get greased. That wheel often gets replaced. The Golden Rule is powerful in its simplicity: treat others as you wish to be treated. A kind word never goes unheard but too often goes unsaid. Instead of looking for ways to knock another person down, the successful and happy person is on the lookout for an opportunity to build another person up.

I feel it's our obligation to also create opportunities for others. Where would we be without the guidance and leadership of our parents, coaches, mentors, and teachers? The words of my father come into play in my life nearly every day. I channel the professional guidance of Bob Barker and Sande Stewart every time I put on the suit and grab the microphone. The list of men and women to whom I am grateful for sharing their experiences in order for me to better myself is far too lengthy to share here. But because of their generosity, I now strive to be a positive influence and a source of guidance for young hosts. Such an opportunity presented itself during a *The Price Is Right Live!* show in late 2014 at Illinois State University's Sangamon Auditorium.

The energy in the theater that evening was indescribable. There are some shows where nothing goes according to plan, but there are others in which everything just seems to click. It's a magical feeling that I don't have the words to describe properly. It's like smelling BBQ ribs grilling on the beach of a tropical island while you receive a scalp massage. Or having Kate Upton show up at your birthday party and ask you to dance while Elton John serenades the two of you with "Sacrifice." Yes, some shows are really *that* good.

The audience of 1700 and I were operating in perfect harmony when a young man named Michael won his way onto the stage to play a pricing game with me. Michael was of average build and dark hair. He was dressed as one might expect a man of his age to be dressed. Nothing out of the ordinary about Michael. During our brief contestant interview, I asked what he was studying at the university.

"Mass communications," he replied.

This opened a mental door for me. Knowing he most likely had a dreams of radio or television, I followed up by asking what he was interested in pursuing after graduation. Michael stated that he would like to one day become a news anchor. The audience cheered in support.

It was evident by the quiver in Michael's upper lip that he hadn't spent much time in front of such a large audience. Not to mention a crowd as fired up as this one was. It was daunting, but those nerves would have to be something he'd need to get over should his dream of hosting the nightly news ever come to fruition. However, no one expected much from him at the tender age of eighteen. Nonetheless, his smile and enthusiasm were clear indicators that he loved every minute of our exchange. This was clearly a moment Michael would remember forever and perhaps even write of one day. I was thrilled to be sharing it with him.

Throughout the history of television, news anchors have been known for their lockouts; signature words or phrases used consistently upon signing off from the airwaves. From Walter Cronkite's "That's the way it is" to Bob Barker reminding us to "...have your pets spayed or neutered," a great sign off has become a staple in the world of local and national broadcast news. It's expected. Michael knew of this well-established tradition and with a bit of cajoling was more than willing to create one for himself right there in front of 3400 watchful eyes.

After some back and forth banter on the stage and little involvement from the first few rows we arrived at a lockout that would be unique to

Michael. We agreed that his goodbye would consist of his name followed by the phrase *Shamalama*.

The absurd verbiage meant nothing to Michael. It meant nothing to anyone. In fact, the awkward collection of syllables was all I could come up with on the spur of the moment to keep the momentum of the show going forward. I wanted Michael to have this moment in time, this memory, but I was also aware we were only midway through the evening's performance and we'd need to get back to the winning sooner rather than later.

At that point I did something I rarely do: I handed the microphone over to Michael. Giving up control of my mic is a risk that normally isn't worth taking because it could lead to disaster in the hands of the wrong person. The inexperienced handler could drop it, run off with it, or break into an obscenity-ladened diatribe against all of humanity. One never knows. But I responded to the looks of concern from our announcer Andy Martello and producer Jim Weathers with a nod of assurance. I trusted Michael and my instincts were telling me to let this situation play out.

Michael received the microphone firmly in his left hand, staring at it as if it might grow fangs and bite him on the nose. He held it so tightly his knuckles were white. He licked his lips and cleared his throat. Staring blindly into the bright spotlight with the look of a child about to dive into the deep end of the swimming pool, he took a breath and fired:

"I'm Michael Lawrence... goodnight and *Shamalama*!"

The audience ate it up. They loved Michael! They even joined him on the *Shamalama* and applauded his bravery. Did the word sound ridiculous reverberating through the auditorium? Of course it did. It's not even a legitimate word and it had no relevance whatsoever to the situation at hand, but I promise you no one will be questioning its origin in twenty years when that young college student is the most respected journalist on television.

Michael's passion for his dream allowed him to work up enough gusto to seize the moment. Carrying him on their proverbial shoulders, the audience propelled him one step further to the realization of his career goal. Standing next to him I could see it all sparkling like a diamond. That was Michael's moment and he seized it

Connecting with the audience should always be a host's primary objective. Everything else is secondary. Through her dancing and conversational approach Ellen DeGeneres has become a master at connecting. Johnny Carson did it. Oprah certainly did it. Phil Donahue did it. Dick Clark did it. Richard Dawson and Gene Rayburn both did it. Even the great baseball play-by-play announcer Harry Caray and radio icon Wolfman Jack, through word choice and delivery, developed unique ways to do it. Regardless of how wealthy they are or what we read about them in the tabloids, good hosts somehow make us feel as if they just stopped by to have a cup of coffee with us. They don't try to be the center of attention, it just seems to work out that way. Establishing that type of rapport has become an unrecognized art form.

Opportunities to connect with an audience, whether it be live, on camera, or on the radio, cannot be concocted. Trying too hard to make something out of nothing or attempting to stick a circle where a square should be only serves to make a host's entire performance appear contrived. Instead, hosts must learn to recognize an opportunity when one presents itself and then begin to massage it into something memorable and enjoyable for the audience.

I previously made mention of Wolfman Jack. Many listeners of the era assumed that distinguishable voice was forced. It was not. Enhanced by a couple of shots of whiskey maybe, but it was the real deal. The wild rock 'n' roll lifestyle that the teenagers of the sixties and seventies were flocking to was who the man was off the air. The Wolfman brought the party because he *was* the party and listeners lived vicariously through him and his antics.

There is a joke in show business that has been around since the discovery of dirt. I believe it dates back to the vaudeville performers who would perform multiple shows daily in places like the Poconos and on the historic boardwalk of Atlantic City. A thousand different performers have told the joke a hundred different ways and it was first introduced to me in 1999 by game show announcer Randy West while working together on my first game show, *Hollywood Showdown*. The line goes something like this:

The Host With The Most

"People often ask me how many people work on this show. I tell them, 'about half of them on a good day."

I decided to dust this oldie-but-goodie off and use it during a *TPIR Live* performance in 2015. Surprisingly, it was well received by the audience. Knowing that there were most likely a few folks who could see the punch line coming from around the corner and down the street, I still chose to throw it out there again the next night and even the night after that. It was on the fourth consecutive night of the joke's abuse that our lighting director, Sam Schwartz, took it upon himself to kill all of the lights as soon as I delivered the finish. His timing was impeccable and the audience ate it up like a three dollar buffet. The dropping of the lights was so out of left field and so perfectly time that I couldn't control my own laughter. The harder I laughed the harder the audience laughed. It was a moment born from instinct and the spontaneity wasn't lost on anyone. We all gathered in my dressing room after the show to slap Sam on the back and sing his praises. It was a brilliant moment that sprouted from absolute purity and we decided to make it a regular bit in the show.

Interestingly enough, the joke didn't go over nearly as well the next night. We were in the same theater in the same city. It came at the exact same moment in the show. The only thing that was different was the genuineness, the realism. Those in attendance seemed able to read that I knew the lights were going to go out. We've hit the joke a few times since but it's never been the killer it was that first time. Maybe I telegraph it a bit or maybe it appears *too* perfect, it's hard to say. What I do know is authenticity cannot be mass produced.

The business of hosting centers around the belief that not only is the moment *for* the audience, it must also be *about* the audience. It is, in its way, very much like a dance; the steps may be the same, but because the partners change it is a different experience each time the music starts.

I vividly recall another instance where the audience fell in love with one of its own. I was hosting a *TPIR Live* performance just outside of San Francisco when a woman in her mid-to-late fifties rose from her seat near the back of the theater and began waving her arms wildly to catch my attention. Normally the spotlight would have been in my face rendering the theater a pool of darkness save for the first three or four rows, but I was standing just off to the side of the stage and my baby blues locked onto her.

"I see you back there, my love," I said for the entire auditorium to hear. "What's on your mind?"

"I want to hug you," she screamed.

It is important to note that any honest-to-goodness game show host will never refuse a hug. We love them! A good squeeze will rev you up better than any energy drink or B12 shot. This is backed up by research found in the journal *Psychological Science* which states that when we embrace someone, oxytocin (also known as "the cuddle hormone") is released. Hugs also have the power to lower blood pressure and reduce the worry of mortality by making us feel safe and loved. What's not to appreciate about that? But my instincts were telling me that this was something more than just a chance to relieve a little stress. This moment had the potential to become something special for her, for me, and for everyone in attendance. It was time to reach into my bag of tricks.

Before hitting the road and touring North America, *TPIR Live* enjoyed a six-year residency at the legendary Bally's Hotel and Casino in Las Vegas. One of the highlights of my career has been driving down Las Vegas Boulevard and seeing my face and name in lights on the world famous marquees in front of Bally's, Harrah's, and Caesars Palace. That is a thrill like none other.

During our successful run in the middle of the Strip, I had the good fortune of forming friendships with several of my fellow Vegas performers. The most legendary of which was "Mr. Las Vegas" himself, Wayne Newton. Contrary to popular belief, we are not related in any way, but Wayne and his wife often invited me to join them for his shows at the Tropicana and even dinner at their extravagant estate, Casa de Shenandoah. The family is so tightly knit that spending time with them often helped me deal with the extreme loneliness that comes from being away from my own children. Eventually, I fell in love with Wayne's beautiful blonde, blue-eyed sister-in-law, Trish. Trish the Dish was, and is, a real stunner who gave me a run for my money in every sense and we shared a delightfully complicated relationship spanning more than two years.

Wayne Newton's live performance is something everyone should see. Few entertainers have more respect for an audience than he does. Wayne comes from a time when a performer left everything on the stage for the fans and still they wanted more. One of his signature moments is finding an adoring fan and bringing her up to give him a kiss on the cheek. Making sure she has a friend in the audience with camera at the ready, he says he'll count to three to make certain the moment is captured. As the giddy, unsuspecting fan prepares to lean in, Wayne counts one... two... then, at the very last moment, turns his head so her lips meet his. The audience member blushes, the audience laughs, and the perfect photo is taken to preserve the moment for eternity.

With Wayne's blessing, I have incorporated a version of the same routine into my performances. Obviously I am not the same type or caliber of entertainer Wayne is, so minor adjustments have been made for optimum results. I explain to the audience that the traditional "game show host kiss on the cheek" was established in 1974 by Richard Dawson (not true) and has been proven to bring good fortune upon all contestants when it is done publicly (also not true). It always brings a laugh and serves as a time filler while the backstage crew makes their transitions behind the curtain.

To be seen as endearing and not come off as creepy, I require two things: the ideal audience member and a breath mint.

The hugger in California seemed perfect. I've learned to trust my hosting instincts over the years and all lights were green as far as she was concerned. I made my way to the back of the theater , took her by the hand, and led her to the center of the aisle to ensure that our cameraman could capture the image of what was about to occur and project it onto the giant screens on either side of the stage.

I explained to her that I'd been away from home for some time and this hug would do my soul some good. This wasn't part of the bit. It was truth. We wrapped our arms around each other, and as she gave me a squeeze, she whispered in my ear, "I love *Whammy*."

"Me too," I replied.

When we had released each other from our embrace, I asked if she would mind serving as my partner in the traditional good luck kiss on the cheek. Without it, I told her, I would feel off balance for the remainder of the show and it would be a shame to deprive the audience of such a proven good luck charm.

The crowd cheered as she obliged. She apparently had come to the show alone so I suggested she pass her smartphone to the man seated next to her who agreed to serve as her photographer. She was going to make the moment special, after all. She deserved to at least have a photo.

I went through my whole spiel about the history of the kiss and the good fortune it delivers. Whether she believed me or not was irrelevant. She had hopped aboard and was ready.

Then, with the spotlight shining down upon us, I bent down just enough to bring my right cheek level with her face. The entire audience counted in unison from one to three, and I turned just in time to engage in a nice lip lock.

As expected, cheers rang out throughout the theater. I hugged her again, thanking her as I prepared to take her back to her seat. Everything seemed to have gone off without a hitch until I noticed tears forming in her eyes. Had I overstepped my boundaries? Had my instincts led me astray? I apologized so only she could hear. Her response broke my heart. "Oh, please don't be sorry. My husband passed away a while back, and that's the first time I've been kissed in more than ten years."

I didn't repeat what she had shared to the crowd. Some things are meant for the masses while others are better kept to an audience of one or two. Perhaps a bit selfishly I chose to keep her words just for myself. Instead, I did what I thought Johnny Carson would've done; I leaned in and kissed her again just for the hell of it.

Over the years, I have kissed hundreds, perhaps even thousands, of women on stages all over the world and each moment was met with applause and a smile. Any age, size, or shape, I don't see anything but the beauty of the moment and that of the individual. We are sharing an experience and taking a ride together. It's show business. Performers at all levels strive to create a bond with their audiences and just as everyone from Wayne to Richard Dawson to Elvis have shown, nothing creates a lasting memory like an innocent little smooch.

Social media provides every type of industry a clear and distinct method with which to gauge feedback in an entirely new and instantaneous manner. In a sense, Twitter, Facebook, Instagram, and review sites have replaced focus groups and ratings services by giving anyone who attends my events or shows the opportunity to go right home and post thoughts and opinions about our time together. Offering individuals the right to share their likes and dislikes in a public forum is a positive thing for the most part, but there are occasions when people seem to climb up on the soapbox only to tear down what you have work so hard to build. Ranting and complaining often result in the only form of attention these people ever receive, but to succeed and continue to grow you cannot let these barking dogs affect your game.

I was enjoying a post show dinner at Seattle's legendary restaurant The Carlile Room when one of our crew members handed me his phone. A woman who had attended that evening's performance had taken offense to the game show kiss routine and posted her disgust on social media. Mind you, it wasn't the woman with whom I shared the kiss nor was it any of the contestants that pecked me on the cheek during the show. It was an audience member who felt the need to speak her mind after the performance had concluded.

The woman also went as far as to seek out one of our producers and explain that at one point in her life she had been a victim of rape and the kiss somehow took her back to that awful event. To her, it felt "sneaky and wrong." I could not believe what I was reading. The further I scrolled through her post the more incensed I became.

The act of physically forcing oneself upon another is despicable and inexcusable. The very thought of it repulses me and I have nothing but the deepest compassion for anyone who has suffered through such an experience. I also have tremendous respect for those who have found the strength within themselves to overcome and regain their deserved happiness. But to compare my actions to such an atrocity deeply offended me.

How dare she think I am so inconsiderate, so carnal, as to incorporate such impropriety into what I do? Had the woman contacted me directly I would have listened intently to her concerns, expressed my sympathy for what she had been through, and then matter-of-factly shared my views on her words.

My instincts told me that this woman had chosen to deal with her tragedy by attempting to rope as many people into her web of sadness as possible. That wasn't necessarily her fault as we all deal with hardship in our own way, but I do not subscribe to the "misery loves company" approach to healing and there certainly wasn't a seat at my table for it. Had she chosen to continue her tirade against me and my performance, I would not have hesitated to file a lawsuit against her for defamation of character. Knowing who and what you are is a must in life. Showing love and understanding for our fellow human beings is necessary for the survival of our species, but we are nothing without integrity. Never, ever allow someone to call your character into question. Protect your brand at all costs.

Hosting, at its core, is about capitalizing on one single, solitary moment at a time. I will repeat that again and again throughout this book. Spotlighting that moment and making it so shiny for everyone involved that we need to squint our eyes to take it all in is vital. It's about creating smiles and inspiring lasting emotion by emphasizing all that is right with the world. It's not so much what we say, but how we make you feel. That is what you'll remember long after the show is over and you've returned to your busy life. Aim to please everyone and accept that if you can connect with the overwhelming majority you've done a pretty good job.

Speaking of ratings and feedback, I returned to my radio roots in 2013 by joining the podcast revolution with *The Todd Newton Show*, followed by *The 30 Minute Week* in early 2015. These weekly productions were exciting for me because they allowed me to broadcast to the entire world via the Internet. Whereas before my listening audience was confined to St. Louis, Los Angeles, New York or whatever city I happened to be working in, listeners could now download episodes on their smartphones, computers, or tablets from anywhere and listen at their leisure.

Another modern benefit of podcasting is that I, as a personality, was no longer required to operate under the watchful eye of the Federal Communications Commission. For the first time in my twenty plus years on the airwaves, my guests and I were free to speak as normal, responsible adults would in everyday conversation. I don't need a government agency holding my hand while I'm on the air. Ethical boundaries are more pronounced in my psyche than legal limitations. Never one to abuse the freedom provided by the First Amendment by cursing inordinately, I feel as if an interviewee on my show should be comfortable with the fact that he or she has been freed from the chains of censorship.

Podcasting has also played directly into my sense of entrepreneurship. On commercial radio I am required to adhere to a programming schedule that told me when I needed to take commercial breaks, wrap up an interview, or end my show. Each hour there would be eight to ten commercials that would interrupt my flow with the audience. Commercial radio stations will never admit this, especially to potential advertisers, but the truth is audiences turn the dial when the commercials begin playing. I don't believe commercial radio is an effective use of an advertising dollar. It has been proven to be *in*effective for a very long time, and there are too many other, more productive, places for a business to spend its money. No longer would any of this be an issue for me. An episode of my podcast could last five minutes, or it could run two hours and those annoying commercials were replaced by short sponsor reads at the top and bottom of the show. Better yet, every dollar spent by those sponsors fell directly into my pocket.

From a performance standpoint, the decision of what would be broadcast out was mine and mine alone to make. I was the best judge as to the type of content I featured on *The Todd Newton Show* and the number of downloads we received each week proved that we had a good grasp on what the audience was expecting and appreciating. Add to all of this the fact that I was able to keep my overhead costs to a minimum by broadcasting from the comfort of my home at the beach and it was clear that podcasting made perfect sense.

In today's marketplace it is essential that hosts build and maintain a brand for themselves. It is the basis of your career. The industry needs to know who you are and what it is you do. Personally, I have taken advantage of one of the greatest tools to come along since the printing press to publicize my work and introduce myself to a broader audience. The Internet not only allows me to present my marketing materials to casting agents and producers in seconds and develop a podcast that is heard globally, but it has made it possible to trademark *The Host with the Most®* as well as *The Celebrity Real Estate Agent®* and allowed me to achieve my goal of becoming an author. None of this means a thing, however, if the audience doesn't feel a connection with you. Great moments provide the foundation for that connection, and hosts should never slow down when it comes to selling themselves. We are the product.

When I step off a stage or when the lights go out on a set, I don't always feel as if the performance I just gave was the best performance ever. They can't all be gems. That night's show may not put another Emmy statue on my mantel or solidify my place in the Broadcasters Hall of Fame, but if there was just one single moment that I know the audience will be talking about later then we can mark it up as a win. There are a million definitions of success, but for me the knowledge that the audience felt something positive; warmth, joy, hilarity, as a result of our time together lets me know I've done my job. It's not the ratings, the number of tickets sold, or the standing ovations; it will always be those special moments that mean the most to me.

CHAPTER 4

Who Are You Supposed To Be?

The balmy Southern California temperatures had finally begun to show some mercy in Los Angeles as autumn attempted to make her presence known. If ever there was a time of year when those on the left coast are envious of those on the right, this would be it as Californians are rarely gifted with the awe-inspiring sight of leaves turning from green to orange.

Having spent my childhood years in Missouri, I am no stranger to the chill an October evening can bring, but the thin-blooded coastal kids busying the sidewalks in front of my home were bundled up as if they were off to explore the frozen tundra. Nothing dilutes the fright of a Halloween costume like a hoodie zipped up to the chin. It's not ghouls, goblins, or bumps in the night sending shivers up their young spines, but rather temperatures threatening to dip below the fifty-five-degree mark.

Halloween, for as far back as my mind will take me, has always been a favorite holiday of mine. The fact that I now have children of my own through whom I can experience the mayhem allows me to enjoy it all over again as an adult.

The year was 2007. Silver and I had just dissolved our marriage and were co-parenting quite successfully. Halloween would be the first holiday I would spend with my children as a single dad. Because of that, I wanted the evening to be special but also have a sense of routine and regularity. I just wanted it to be fun.

After weeks of discussion and careful deliberation, my son chose to hit the streets dressed as a SWAT Team member. A friend of mine in Las Vegas had recently arranged for Mason and me to visit her husband, a real SWAT team member, on the job. As a result of our father/son excursion, my boy was aware of every component necessary to legitimize his outfit: helmet, plastic billy club, camouflage face paint, even the authentic law enforcement terminology he picked up from meeting the guys became part of the costume. The only accessory that could've made his outfit more realistic was a set of steel handcuffs. In my sporadic parental wisdom, I deemed these a not-so-great idea.

My daughter chose to be a Native American princess. Her school-made headband adorned with multi-colored feathers provided the cutest contrast to her blonde locks, which her mother had meticulously braided.

Did I choose to partake in the festivities, you ask? Considering the fact that bobbing for apples strikes me as highly unsanitary and that I've never been sold on the existence of ghosts, I chose to indulge in the revelry by fulfilling a certain fantasy.

After seeing the band KISS in concert no more than three weeks prior, I opted to adorn a black rock n roll wig and meticulously apply the coveted face paint of The Starchild, Paul Stanley. One of the great front men in rock history, Paul controls hordes of adoring and loyal fans with the precision of an orchestra conductor. I've learned many tricks of the trade from observing Paul live and will occasionally throw a few of his lines into a show or presentation I'm doing.

Our plans for trick or treating called for us to take a short walk along the famed Ventura Boulevard and meet up with some of the other neighborhood kids. Occasionally I would receive a nod of appreciation from a fellow KISS fan. Though my costumes often embarrassed my kids, I knew that one day they would appreciate the fact that Dad just wanted to be in it with them. Again, it's all about making the memories.

The sun was still setting in the San Fernando Valley as the streetlights began to flicker on. Cars proceeded down the congested side streets with extra caution as countless SpongeBobs, Disney princesses, and Transformers hustled those brave enough to answer their doors with schoolyard jokes in exchange for Sour Patch Kids and fun-sized Snickers.

Walking door-to-door can become tiring when you are not the one replenishing your sugar intake at every stop. This becomes especially true after the ninth or tenth block. While the kids took a breather and compared their takes, the dads and I pulled out our smartphones and compared photos we had taken throughout the evening.

Amidst the yapping and candy unwrapping, the sound of my son's voice seemed to rise above the noise as he posed a question to one of the young girls in our group. It was an innocent enough question, but I knew as soon as the last word left his mouth that it would become the title of a chapter in my next book.

"Who are you supposed to be?"

Our neighbor huffed in disgust and frustration before responding that she was a punk rocker. Pointing out her colored hairspray, scuffed combat boots, and multi-colored fingernail polish as if she were admitting evidence in a court of law, she was giving my son his first dose of female sass. His poignant question, however, made me stop for a moment and ponder how, on this one night, all of mankind is allowed to dress up and act like someone (or something) that we are not but perhaps wish we could be.

Every year on October 31st, we are permitted to dress, act, and speak in whatever manner or fashion we choose and it is accepted by everyone we encounter. No matter how far away from our reality or costume may take us, there are no doubts or insecurities associated with the transformation.

Take a moment right now to ask yourself the question my son asked of his little friend: Who are *you* supposed to be? Are you supposed to be doing the job you're currently doing? How would you act if you wanted to be a better parent, more productive employee, or more respected member of your community? Suppose your doorbell rang and you answered it only to find someone acting like you. Would you approve?

I know that if I encountered a "me" on Halloween I would want to be proud of what I saw. I'd hope only the best of my features would be showing while the worst of me got left behind. I hope others would want to be around him. And I hope he would willingly share his Reese's Peanut Butter Cups with those who had been stuck with nickels or fruit.

If I were anything but a host I would be miserable. I am only able to wake up at 3 a.m. to work out because I want my suits to fit properly. I only read the books I read because the words either benefit me professionally or entertain me personally. I can only stand to go out on the road and be away from my family because they understand that making people happy on stage and television is what Dad does for a living. And he loves it.

I encourage you to take this moment and think about the costume you're wearing today. Is it who you are supposed to be? If it's not, that may be the root of many of the challenges you're currently facing in your life. There is no upside to carrying on in a state of unhappiness. You do yourself and your family a great disservice by shortchanging them of the magic that is a fulfilled and authentic you. Don't ever be timid when it comes to reaching for all that you deserve. Never allow your fears to immobilize you. Successful people go for it. They take chances. They slide all of their chips to the middle of the table.

If changes need to be made to your outfit, make them. Don't expect to be granted permission and don't wait for acceptance. You don't need it and you probably wouldn't find it. Instead, tap into some of that Halloween magic and carry it with you each day. Step up your game by dressing, speaking, and acting the part you know you are meant to play. Follow your heart and trust your instincts. You'll be amazed at how comfortable you feel in your new role.

And while you're at it, take the time to share the most important "treats" in life. Honesty, loyalty, compassion, peace, and love don't come in a wrapper and you don't need to wait for them to go on sale November 1st. They're available to you right now… and they won't melt in your hands!

CHAPTER 5

Services Rendered. Pay the Man

Certain clichés are so ingrained and so often repeated that they sound meaningful even when they hold no water whatsoever. All too often we blindly buy into the nonsense. Repetition builds reputation. "You can lead a horse to water but you can't make him drink," is a real stretch. I've spent a little time around horses and have never found it to be much of a battle when you walk a thirsty horse to a cold trough on a hot day.

"It's easier said than done" is a recognized saying. Anyone can project a need or a want, but very few possess the ability to follow it through to fruition. Words without action are just noise. People get bored, distracted, or frustrated and abandon whatever it is they initially set out to accomplish. That particular task then appears even harder for the next person who attempts it and so on down the line.

Early in my professional life, I was much more of a pushover than I am today. I won't say I was ever taken advantage of, but I was certainly softer around the edges and less hardened by time and experience. My goal was always to be easy to work with and a pleasure to be around. But as the years have passed, I have learned a thing or two and now I have a tendency to focus a little more on my own comforts as opposed to accommodating the needs of others.

I was not far into my radio career when I began to get a taste for the finer things in life. At the age of nineteen, I moved out of my parents' home and in with an older woman named Debbie. We shared a wonderful little apartment in south St. Louis and I embraced the responsibilities that accompanied my new foray into adulthood. Our relationship was an invaluable learning experience for me. With Debbie, I discovered the concept of *we* instead of just *me*. It was a real transition and the growing pains felt good.

But with all that Debbie and I were sharing, I began discovering things about myself and how relationships worked. As much as I tried to ignore certain natural urges, I was still a young man with a young man's needs. I didn't yet have the maturity to be deserving of Debbie's trust and I let the temptations of radio fame overtake the security of being one-half of a real couple. My last memory of us together involves picking my clothes up off the back lawn and stuffing them into a white trash bag before driving off in search of a new place to live.

Breakups can be sad, but they also mean new beginnings. I didn't sulk over the dissolution of our two-year affair for long, and I have never backtracked on any relationship. I do not believe in getting back together with someone whom I have decided to part ways with or who no longer has a need for me. It's onward and upward, so I reacted to the separation the only way I could think of: by signing a lease on a ridiculously large and remarkably overpriced apartment.

My new place was a bachelor's paradise. Hardwood floors and arched doorways met the dark oak and floor-to-ceiling windows giving the place a majestic feel that I still seek when I purchase property today. I believe in paying for the things I want as long as it doesn't jeopardize the things I need.

Though I would never consider myself a careless spender, I also cannot be labeled as frugal. I am a calculated investor, an aggressive saver, and a wise spender. You will never see me throwing money away on careless vices such as alcohol or gambling, but it is not uncommon for me to pick up and fly to Europe on a whim. I pay for experiences, not extravagances.

There is much more to the radio industry than what meets the ear. The voices you listen to in your car have duties that far exceed playing your favorite songs or dishing on your favorite topics four hours a day. To maintain our place in the market and earn our spot on your dial, we must continuously stay on top of what's happening both locally and nationally, work the social media outlets, and hit the streets to establish our relevance.

More often than not, the base salary of a radio personality is not enough to live the lives we want to live. To supplement our streams of revenue jocks must also produce commercials, pitch clients for endorsements, and appear in person at car dealerships, state fairs, and nightclubs.

Fortunately, I no longer do many appearances on behalf of radio stations. This was not always the case, of course. As a young DJ coming up the ranks, I would have shown up at the opening of a garage door if you paid me enough. I've handed out more bumper stickers and radio station t-shirts than I care to recall, but you would never hear me complain as long as my name was spelled correctly on the check. Saying 'no' had never been a problem for me personally or socially, but professionally I was defenseless when it came to an opportunity to earn a dollar. My desire to please had a tendency to get me into some awkward situations.

As mentioned in an earlier chapter, my entrée into the wonderful word of radio came about from an opportunity to work overnights at a local St. Louis Top 40 station known as KHTK HOT 97. Before taking control of the microphone, I had served as an intern, thanklessly doing everything from alphabetizing cassette tapes and CD's to washing the station van in the parking lot. But my willingness to work for little or no pay brought massive returns in the end.

Success often falls upon those who hold on a little longer than everyone else and one day my ship came into port when one of the DJ's overslept and missed her shift. In the world of radio this was an unforgivable sin and there I was, like a batter taking practice swings in the on-deck circle, ready to step up to the plate. I'd like to say I knocked it out of the park during that first shift but that wouldn't be entirely true. If I begin to think that I am perfect or flawless I have nothing to challenge myself with. For that reason I will conservatively say I hit an easy ground rule double during my first performance.

It takes a village to make a radio station function effectively. Salespeople, programmers, management, and talent each do their share for the greater good. Alice Ross was our hard-nosed sales manager who knew how to squeeze every dollar out of a client and then make him say thank you. Even during my tenure at Home Shopping Network, I did not master the art of the upsell the way Alice had.

Alice immediately took advantage of my youthful good looks and enthusiasm by marketing me as the fresh face of the radio station. Much to the chagrin of the more seasoned personalities, I became the guy who was lining his pockets with appearance money even though most listeners had no idea who I was or what I sounded like on the air.

My first solo live broadcast took place in a mall food court on a busy Saturday afternoon before Christmas. As shoppers made their way from one retail chain outlet to the next in search of the perfect gift, I sat nervously behind a table draped with a station cover playing the day's most popular hits and encouraging folks of all ages to stop by and sign up for the hot dog decorating contest that I would be judging later that day. I was humiliated and exhilarated at the same time. While most of my high school buddies were suffering through construction jobs in the summer heat, I was sitting in an air-conditioned shopping center wearing a Decorate Your Dog baseball cap. It was not the glamorous showbiz lifestyle one might associate with working on the radio in a major market, but I was getting paid $100/hour and for that kind of money I would've worn just about any hat they asked me to put on.

Soon, at the behest of Alice, our sales representatives began pushing me on car dealerships, theme parks, and nightclubs. I was better on the microphone than most of the old veterans because the business had not yet turned me bitter and enthusiasm translates to energy when you're in front of the crowd. The others had lost it while I had just discovered it. My excellent head of hair and bright, white teeth made me a favorite with the female demographic over the middle-aged, paunchy voices St. Louis had grown weary of.

I wisely began to re-invest some of the money I was making into my new image. Purchasing new clothes, treating myself to manicures and pedicures, and driving a few extra miles to visit the trendiest hair salons became the cost of doing business for me and it did not take long to being seeing the returns. Within a few short months teenagers began waiting in line for my autograph and professional women would linger to give me their business cards.

In February of 1992, I signed a contract to host the more respected 10am-2pm air shift. The new time slot meant my voice would now be heard for more than twenty hours a week in the city I had lived in all of my life. I spoke the language of the people and was now speaking primarily to that coveted demographic of women 25-54 years of age. This was who either earned all the money in the household or was in charge of spending all of the money in the household. Either way, I wanted them. I didn't just want them to listen to me on the radio, I wanted to become a part of their day. I wanted to give them an on-air product that was so polished and personable that the first thing they did when they got into their car, before they even fastened their seatbelt, was tune me in on the FM dial. Though there were viable alternatives, I wanted the average woman to forget about every other radio station she had ever listened to and focus on me, my voice, and our music. I had all they needed. They just needed to know it.

Radio is fascinating in the sense that we hear the same voices day after day yet aren't always able to feel connected to the man or woman we are listening to. They are merely background noise. That is not the fault of the listener; it's the fault of the personality. Often it boils down to the fact that the host or personality speaks *at* the audience as opposed to *to* or *with* the audience. That is an instant turn off for me. My process of connecting was taught to me by some of the jocks on our sister station who seemed to be almost idolized by their listeners.

SOUL 63 was an AM radio station in town that played the R&B and Motown hits of days gone by. The station enjoyed a loyal audience that was limited in size by its weak signal, but the air staff was wall-to-wall superstars. SOUL 63's studio was connected to that of my station, HOT 97, by a door with a small window that I would often peer through to watch local legends like "Gentleman Jim" Gates and "The Real JR" work their on-air magic. Jim, in particular, had a voice so smooth you'd swear it could cut butter. His dulcet tones rivaled those of Barry White and we'd often refer to him as "Genitals Jim" around the station because of the jealousy we felt. I once asked him if he could teach me how to dig as deeply as he did for his voice and he said, "I love ya, Toddy, but white boys just don't have the balls for it."

JR, on the other hand, was more of a character who somehow managed to hold gingerly the entire urban population of St. Louis in the palm of his hand. People loved him because he localized so well. JR would talk about Norma in Hazelwood's new car or seeing Denise from Belleville at the bank that morning. He gossiped, griped, and flirted his way through each and every show he did and people loved it.

JR would frequently come parading into the station wearing an obnoxiously large cowboy hat and carrying a tray of food that a local restaurant had given him just for stopping in. A towering figure of six feet six inches tall, he was the man about town and played his image to the hilt.

A couple of months into my new shift, I was just beginning to feel settled in my role. My co-workers were beginning to accept me and the ratings were on the rise. Alice came into the studio to tell me about a new nightclub that had opened its doors on Washington Ave, a four block strip in the heart of downtown St. Louis. Today Washington is thriving with lofts filled with trendy young people, coffee shops, and craft beer distilleries. But in the nineties, the rent was dirt cheap for a reason. After the law offices and department stores had closed shop for the day, the area became a crime-ridden ghost town.

To open a live music venue in such a desolate area was a real risk financially, but Alice Ross convinced the owner, a gruff, middle-aged African American man with a nasty attitude toward women, that a live broadcast with SOUL 63 would not only fill the place but also establish his joint as the new hotspot in town. The owner agreed on one condition: the Real JR would be the personality on hand. Immediately Alice knew she had him. The deal was all but signed when Alice took advantage of her leverage and went one step further.

Alice explained that JR was not only expensive, but he didn't much care to promote new establishments. The fact that the owner wanted to focus on the late-night crowd and didn't want his broadcast to begin until 1 a.m. made things even more difficult because, as Alice explained, JR would need to get his rest before going on the air the next morning. But after seeing the disappointment in the old man's eyes, perhaps she could talk JR into it if the radio station's side of the deal became a little sweeter.

What if, Alice proposed, the event became a double broadcast with SOUL 63's sister station, HOT 97, and she threw St. Louis' newest DJ (me) into the deal? Now he'd be attracting the upscale urban crowd from the city as well as the suburbanites who were always craving someplace new to spend their money. It was a brilliant maneuver on Alice's part. I'm always awed by the skill set of a strong negotiator. Somehow Alice was able to double the advertising revenue for the station, secure a talent fee for JR, and come up with an unexpected chunk of change for me all during lunch. A triple Whammy.

I will admit to being slightly apprehensive after learning of the upcoming appearance. Not only would it be the first time I had been placed in front of a primarily black audience, but it was also my first live late show. Being tucked away in the coziness of a small radio studio at 2 a.m. is one thing, but trying to maintain and elevate the energy of a crowded dance floor at that hour was something entirely different. I was accustomed to firing up large crowds of teenagers at 7 p.m. so they could make it home by curfew and now I was being thrown on a stage at a time when the rest of the world slept. The flow would be new to me, but not to JR.

JR and I shared a mutual respect for one another. Much like the friendship I'd enjoyed with Jimmy Paige years before, I posed no threat to his listenership so I was not viewed as a competitor. Radio can be brutal at times. Put two disc jockeys from competing stations in the same room and one is guaranteed to walk out badly bruised, but this wasn't the case between JR and myself. Instead, I latched onto him. I asked if he would mind meeting me in the parking lot so we could walk in together. I hoped to gain the crowd's acceptance through osmosis. I knew they loved JR, so maybe this kid with him wouldn't be so bad either. Whether or not JR was aware of my plan I can't say for sure, but he agreed to go along with it. So, shortly before we were scheduled to go on stage and cut the ribbon on the new nightclub, I strutted through the front door with JR on one side and my beautiful blonde girlfriend on the other. In hindsight, it may have been a bit too showy. These folks may not leave in the morning loving me, but they would have to admit that I knew how to make an entrance.

Dark. That's really all I remember of my first impression of the place. It was really, really dark. I also recall the club having very low ceilings and multi-colored lights. It was slow going at the beginning of the night, but as the hours ticked away attendance began to build. I've never been a late-night kind of guy, but I respect the fact that there is a large market for the after-hours scene. There's a lot of money to be made once the more mainstream bars and nightclubs turn off their neon lights. By midnight I was fighting off the yawns, but a part of me was glad to be grabbing a piece of the action.

JR flashed his big grin as men and women approached him throughout the evening. He'd hug the ladies and shake hands with the men, somehow remembering all of their names. Every so often he would wave me over from across the room and introduce me to someone as if they were royalty. I saw a pattern to the hierarchy and soon caught on to who the key people to know were. There were musicians, local politicians, and even drug dealers commingling and moving to the same music. Everyone seemed to know one another and I couldn't quite understand why JR and I were even brought in. Clearly word had gotten out about the new club and the patrons were enjoying themselves. The place didn't seem to need any promotion and it certainly wasn't benefitting from my presence. Looking back, I believe it was nothing more than an ego stroke for the owner. He wanted to be a part of JR's world. Even so, I was being paid to be there and I would see it through.

JR excused himself from the small, round cocktail table my girlfriend and I were sharing. I followed him with my eyes as he disappeared through an unmarked door near the fire exit against the back wall. Once again I was alone. I went to the bar and ordered a couple of drinks while I waited for some sort of instruction as to what was expected of me. This wasn't the type of place you'd find a dance contest or lip sync competition and the clientele didn't look the type to want a skinny white boy interrupting their music. I was just about to ask the bartender where I might find the manager when JR came out of the office and made his way back to us.

"Listen here," he said. "I'm going to go up and welcome everyone and thank them for coming out. You just stand next to me. That's all. You don't have to say a word."

I suggested that I should, at least, introduce myself and mention HOT 97. Getting your station call letters out into the streets was a big deal before the Internet and social media. Word of mouth was all we had and I'd hate to think of the tongue lashing I'd get from Alice and the other station executives if they heard I hadn't even touched the microphone. "No, man. Just relax and let me handle everything. Don't worry about a thing." JR responded. I knew at that point this was going to be the longest two hours of my blossoming career.

JR and I walked on stage and he did everything he said he would do. Most of the people weren't even paying attention. They were wrapped up in their own conversations. When a man is talking to a beautiful woman in a dimly lit room, the last thing he is going to do is turn away from her. Anyone who has ever been in front of an audience accepts this. I'm the same way as an audience member. JR just plowed through his rap like he was center stage at Madison Square Garden. When he was through he patted me on the back and exited stage right where he was met by one of the most beautiful women I'd ever seen in person. She had thick, flowing black hair and the smoothest ebony skin imaginable. Her body must have been poured into that little black dress. She gave me a wink and a smile as she turned and sauntered off with the big man.

I've never felt as invisible as I did that night. When I say no one approached me, I mean *no one*. It was an uneasy feeling for someone so accustomed to being the center of attention in almost any setting. Thankfully, Debbie had agreed to accompany me, but even the free drinks we were offered weren't enough to keep her occupied and she was more than a little put off by the meaningless wink from JR's companion. She kept asking me to dance but I refused. Dancing just isn't my thing. I've slow danced with only a handful of women in my life and each time meant something. I was already uncomfortable just being there and had no intention of humiliating myself further by taking to the dance floor and revealing how little rhythm I have. The more I said no the more withdrawn she became. When you're dating the new, up-and- coming DJ in town I guess you have certain expectations, and those expectations were far from being met that night. I knew I was letting her down, but the later it got the less I cared. I just wanted to go home.

Time may appear to pass slowly on occasion, but it never really stops. Eventually three o'clock rolled around and it was time to put an end to the appearance and the madness surrounding it. Alice never should have booked me at that place and that experience is one reason why I am so particular about where I'll appear and what I will do today. My philosophy is to exceed a client's or audience's expectations in whatever I do. I want to give them more bang for their buck than anyone else so I am the first one they think of when they have more money to spend. I definitely thrive on over-delivering, but I had fallen way short in downtown St. Louis. I hadn't impressed anyone, especially Debbie. Nonetheless, I had shown up as promised and made myself available. If all that was asked of me was to stand against the wall and drink Diet Coke all night then so be it. There are worse ways to pay the bills. But I still needed to get paid.

The A.W.E. Effect has taught me that it's good business to collect your money in advance. The modern convenience of transferring funds makes it standard practice today, but that has not always been the way things are done. Nothing makes a host or personality look less professional than to see him or her chasing down a paycheck. It's tacky and disrespectful, but in the nineties there wasn't a choice. There was no direct deposit or PayPal, in fact it was usually cash exchanging hands in the back office. I assumed this night would be no different.

JR must have had an internal clock because he and his lady friend returned at the stroke of three. Where they had been occupying themselves I do not know, but I'm certain they were enjoying a greater degree of privacy than I was. I just wanted to get my money and get out of there. JR, however wanted one more dance. That one song turned into two and then to three as my frustration grew. I didn't want to dampen his swagger, but I also didn't want to be there all night so I finally swung the bat and asked my date to dance. It was the only way I would get JR's attention. "I'm ready to get the hell out of here, brother," I said.

"Then scoot," he replied.

"We need our money."

What JR said next threw me for a loop. "He already paid up, baby!"

The sleazy owner had paid JR as soon as we walked in the door but had been avoiding me all night long. I pulled Debbie off the floor and put two and two together. I was getting stiffed and it didn't appear there was anything I could do about it. I knew I could just leave and let the radio station handle it during regular business hours, but anyone with an ounce of common sense knows that once you leave the scene you're handing over your power. I wanted my two hundred dollars and I had no intention of going home without it.

There was no doubt in my mind that the owner was holed up in his office. All night long I had watched women walk in and out of there. The same bartender that had been flooding my date with vodka cranberries had been personally delivering drinks to the door from the moment we walked in. I'd even watched JR himself visit the sacred room earlier in the evening. God only knows what was taking place back there, but I knew there was no shortage of money exchanging hands, and now it was my turn to line my pockets.

My knocking was more forceful than it needed to be, but the banging that nearly bruised my knuckles was fueled by genuine anger and the need to be heard over the music. My relentless pounding, however, was met with utter silence. I was becoming more and more furious. Whoever was on the other side of that door knew that I was trying to gain their attention but made a conscious effort to ignore me. In fact, at one point, I could've sworn I heard snickering. The situation was spiraling out of control very quickly but I was not going to be the sucker. As young and naive as I was at the time, I knew you do not get between a dog and his meat. That bastard had something that belonged to me and I was going to get it. I'd been made to feel like the butt of the joke all night long, but now the party was over. Two hundred dollars is two hundred dollars.

As much as I may have wanted to, I could not just kick in the door and rough the owner up until he forked the money over. First of all, kicking in doors only happens in the movies. Secondly, the gentlemen working security at the club would have had me for lunch. Each one outweighed me by an easy one hundred and fifty pounds. I needed to take a deep breath and use some logic to achieve my desired outcome.

JR had one foot out the door when I managed to push my way through the crowd and catch him. His lady friend did not look so happy to see me now. The two of them had plans for one another and I didn't like holding up their adult party games, but this qualified as an emergency. "JR, he paid you but he's trying to stiff me," I explained, attempting to keep the desperation out of voice. "He's locked himself back in the office."

"You sure you didn't get paid at the top?" he asked.

"Positive. I know I didn't bring much to the table and this was your crowd, but a deal is a deal."

"Son of a bitch," JR said. I could see the anger rising within him. "Wait here, baby. Todd you follow me," and together we made our way to back of the club.

By now I was getting scared. I couldn't see this situation turning out any way but ugly. When we got to the door that had served as my whipping post for the past forty-five minutes, I stood back and expected JR to begin knocking. To my surprise, he just casually reached down and turned the knob. The door had not been locked in the first place. Those in the circle felt comfortable simply walking right in. I guess that explained the chuckling I'd heard earlier, but there was nothing funny about the situation we walked into.

The tiny room was overflowing with inebriated revelers. I could smell it. The scent of whiskey on someone's breath still takes me back to that night in the way only an aroma or a song can do. In my mind's eye, I can see three ladies sprawled out on leather couches that lined each wall. These women were someone's daughters and they were being treated like nothing more than window dressing. Five men trying their best to look like players wore inexpensive, loud-colored suits while leaning against filing cabinets and smoking Kool cigarettes. All eyes turned to JR and me. You could feel the energy shift almost immediately. The owner sat behind a large wooden desk. Stacks of cash were placed neatly before him as he counted the night's take.

"Show's over, boys. Get on home," he barked. The others laughed.

"We appreciate you having us, that's for sure," JR said through his trademark smile. "But Todd says you forgot something. His money."

"Todd drank my booze with the blonde all night. That makes us even. Now get out and shut the door."

"I was drinking Diet Coke…" JR threw his hand up to silence me.

Approaching the desk, JR stood up straighter than I'd ever seen a man stand. I thought for sure his head was going to break through the ceiling. The thugs in leisure suits now came to attention and began to close in. I started to wonder if what was happening was really worth the dollar amount we were discussing, but it was too late to turn back now. Things were in motion. I was shaking in my boots, genuinely fearful for my health, but JR had the poise and confidence of a man in complete control.

The owner slowly raised is bloodshot eyes to him. It was hard to gauge what was going through his sweaty, bald head. Clearly he was not used to being confronted in such a way and did not take kindly to being disrespected in his own place and in front of the ladies. This was evolving into one of those situations where the wrong move could cost you more than you're willing to pay. My father was right when he preached nothing good happens after midnight.

"The boy was here on time. Smiling his ass off. Makin' folks look good," JR was really selling me. "That's what he does and what I do. And it doesn't matter what his lady drank. That's the business, baby. You know that I know that."

Next came a line that I knew I would recall, recite, and relive again and again for the rest of my life.

"Services rendered... *pay the man!*"

JR, still towering over the man, stared into his eyes for what seemed like a lifetime. They were ugly, heartless eyes. No one in the room moved a muscle. Even the menthol scented smoke seemed to cease its swirling as an awful stillness overtook us all.

We all jumped with a start as the owner sliced the tension with a quick slide of his hand. The move was too sudden for the situation and he knew it. With a smirk that revealed his yellow stained teeth, he reached into the top drawer of his old, battered desk. Thinking he might be reaching for a gun, I eased my way behind JR. I've found that bravery has a tendency to take a backseat to survival when firearms are involved, but what he pulled out was not a pistol. It was an envelope filled with cash. He threw it at me and it bounced off my chest before falling to the floor. Twenty dollar bills fanned out at my feet. I have decent hands, but in my defense I didn't see it coming. Pride had been eluding me since the moment I pulled up to this smoky gin joint, but now that I had my money I wanted to regain at least a morsel of my dignity. I bent down to pick up the envelope and slowly counted the cash as if I wouldn't leave until I confirmed it was all there.

It doesn't take long to count to two hundred by twenty. I sealed the envelope so as not to drop a note and said, "Thank you very much." JR was close on my heels as we walked out of the office. "Just keep walking toward the door," he said. "Don't slow down." I took an enraged Debbie by the hand and didn't take a breath until we were safely in my car and cruising westbound on I-44.

The next day, I walked into the SOUL 63 studio and thanked JR for standing up for me. Not only had he risked getting his ass kicked in an environment where the players make the rules, but he had risked his reputation in the nightclub world. JR taught me that you can't put a price tag on integrity. You do what is right no matter the cost and you become invaluable and respected as a result.

It's been over twenty-five years and the little club has long since closed its doors. JR and I have both gone on to make enough money that the stipend we received on that memorable night now seems like little more than a story you'd tell at a cocktail party, but I'd still stand up for JR and repay that debt any day. You never really know what turn a business deal will take, and you need to be prepared to defend yourself and your reputation in any situation.

Foxwoods Casino in Connecticut is an amazing spectacle. The way it seems to appear magically through the trees as you drive along the small New England road leading up to it is something straight out of a fairytale. The accommodations are first rate, the many restaurants offer something for all tastes, and the nine million square feet of gaming make traveling across the country to gamble in Las Vegas a thing of the past. Add to these luxuries the incredible entertainment that the resort brings in and you have a destination that has changed the casino industry for the better.

I first had the opportunity to perform at Foxwoods in 2007. Since then I have performed, hosted, or presented on the majestic property many times and often fly my parents in to enjoy its many amenities with me. Many casinos I find myself in provide enough to keep me busy that I do not feel the need to even step outside. I find myself going two or three days without seeing the sun or taking a breath of natural air. Foxwoods is different. Regardless of the time of year, I make it a point to take advantage of the trails surrounding the beautiful grounds. I also enjoy hopping in the car for a trip to the nearby town Mystic. There are few things more relaxing in the middle of a busy week of shows than enjoying a hot cup of pumpkin spice coffee by the water or a stroll through one of the locally owned shops.

I've been called many things: boisterous, aggressive, a workaholic, but one thing I've never been mistaken for is a party animal. What I do enjoy after putting in a solid day of work is a nice dinner. I believe a good meal is a worthy reward for a job well done. Spoiling my taste buds and experiencing the atmosphere that accompanies fine dining is a real treat for me. I may not always remember the hotel I stayed in or the airport I left from, but I can usually point you the best steak or homemade lasagna in any city you may find yourself in. When I am at Foxwoods, Shrine stands above all the rest.

Shrine offers some of the best sushi I have discovered in New England. The ambiance was ideal whether I was having drinks with a lady friend or dinner with business associates. As the night went on, the restaurant evolves into one of the more popular nightclubs in the area, featuring top live acts and DJs. Only once did I stay late enough to see just how much things heated up when the sun went down.

Throughout the nineties, I had a very casual relationship with a woman named Michelle. I've always found redheads with blue eyes particularly alluring and Michelle fit the bill. Add to that her incredible sense of humor and the fact that her father was one of the greatest actors in cinematic history and you can well understand why I enjoyed spending time with her.

Michelle and I met well before Silver and I were married. Once Silver came along, I became blind to every other woman on Earth and remained that way until our divorce. Infidelity was never an issue for us. We were solid, faithful partners and still are in some respects. But shortly after I returned to bachelorhood, Michelle and I found ourselves back in touch. She mentioned that she was going to be in New York and asked if I'd like to have dinner in Connecticut as it had been many years since we'd seen each other. I had no one else in my life at the time and took things one step further by asking her to join me for the weekend at Foxwoods. It seemed wasteful to be enjoying an extravagant hotel suite alone when I could be sharing it with someone with whom I felt comfortable and had once shared an intense chemistry.

It seemed as if no time had passed when I met Michelle at the New London train station. She had not aged a bit and was the same free-spirited young lady I had enjoyed being with many years before. We were happy to be in each other's company again and the opportunity to spend a couple of days re-igniting the physical flame that burned between us was something we both were apparently looking forward to.

Sadly, the moment for Michelle to return to the project she was working on in New York arrived much sooner than either of us would've liked it to. Time flies when when you're wearing fluffy bathrobes and ordering room service. I suggested we say goodbye with a nice dinner at Shrine after my Sunday show.

The food was exquisite, the martinis were dirty, and the conversation was reminiscent of the many late nights we spent together in the trendiest spots Hollywood had to offer during our younger days. When the server left to settle our bill. I excused myself to use the restroom.

Shrine's music had become noticeably louder and more up tempo. I noticed the clientele had shifted from couples seeking a quiet dinner to the younger crowd seeking love and lust amongst the Buddhist decor. I was just wrapping up my business in the men's room when the door opened and in strolled a very attractive woman. My first thought was that perhaps she'd had one too many and accidentally entered the wrong restroom. This assumption was immediately put to rest when she saw me and said, "I thought that was you."

"Excuse me?"

"I was at your show tonight and noticed you when you walked by my table. Then I saw you walk in here," she explained, as if following a game show host into the toilet was an everyday occurrence.

By this point, my main focus was getting my pants snapped and my belt buckled. The last thing I needed was for someone to walk in and assume that things were what they definitely seemed to be. That would take more explaining than I was prepared to do after a big dinner. Fortunately, a Shrine security guard had spotted her coming in and had by now made his way to where our chance meeting was growing more uncomfortable by the second.

I tip my hat to the way he handled the situation. He politely held the door open for her and asked her to leave. He even went as far as to offer her a complimentary drink at the bar; a tactic commonly used in upscale establishments as a means to avoid confrontation. I was grateful to him for acting so delicately and thanked him profusely. We still had two weeks' worth of performances at the casino and I didn't want to make any waves.

A semi-shy grin made its way to my face as I replayed the brief encounter to myself. I couldn't wait to return to my table and share what had just occurred with Michelle. This would, no doubt, be a story we'd reflect on the next time fate chose to bring us together. What I didn't realize at the time was that part two of the saga was yet to unfold.

No sooner had I finished washing my hands and tossing a buck to the bathroom attendant than the door to the restroom opened again. Much like on the show *Let's Make A Deal* it was anyone's guess who or what was on the other side. I don't think I'd fare very well on the TV show because I received the ultimate *Zonk!* Standing before me, in the exact spot my female admirer had occupied just moments earlier, was her husband!

The enraged gentleman had stormed into the bathroom like a man on a mission. Spittle flew from his lips as he screamed, "I saw you pull my wife in here. Where is she?" There was no time for words. He wasn't there to gather my side of things and there clearly was no room to reason. He was there to do battle with the man who he believed had challenged his honor. I was just there to have a few spicy tuna rolls with a screen legend's daughter.

It had been a while since I'd had to defend myself in a physical altercation. One assumes that after a certain age those occurrences grow further and further apart before disappearing altogether. By applying the A.W.E. Effect and concluding that it's always better just to walk away, one is often able to avoid a world of headaches and save a mountain of money in litigation fees. In a world plagued by lawsuits and false accusations, I believe it's easier in the long run to smile and say goodnight. My pride and self-esteem are not gauged by the thoughts and words of others. This man, however, was leaving me no choice. He was a legitimate threat and I reacted accordingly by squaring myself up and raising my fists to just below my face. We were relatively the same size, but I had the advantage of sobriety.

The first punch of the round was a telegraphed right hook that missed its mark by a country mile. Now he was not only stupid and drunk but also embarrassed and vulnerable. I watched his core movements and could tell he was not an experienced fighter. He was a barroom bully at best and I now had his number. Still, I could not afford to underestimate him and take a shot to the face that might potentially leave me with a black eye or a busted lip. Even the smallest laceration would be tough to explain to producers, promoters, and especially to audiences.

The man's biggest mistake was allowing himself to succumb to desperation. I had yet to throw a single punch but he was already winded. His last attempt at putting me out was a lame head butt. Because of the liquor, he was moving slowly and every action was exaggerated. I saw him draw his head way back and attempt to line me up in his blurred vision. What little martial arts and boxing training I've had taught me that a solid head butt needs to be a quick, whipping motion that ideally connects the attacker's forehead to the bridge of the opponent's nose. When properly executed it's a devastating maneuver that can end just about any conflict.

As the irate husband lunged toward me in a final attempt to put me down for the count, his forehead was met with my right fist. The velocity of our body parts rushing together and meeting in the middle created an impact that nearly knocked him off his feet while almost shattering my knuckles. Feeling as if my hand may be broken, I managed to hit him one final time for good measure. I was certainly within the parameters of self-defense and needed to ensure my safety by making sure he wouldn't attempt another attack until security could once again come to my rescue.

I cannot say with any degree of certainty how long this little escapade lasted, but it was long enough to cause Michelle to worry. As she would later recall, she came looking for me and was met by a man stumbling out of the restroom with blood streaming from his nose. Unable to believe her eyes, she claimed that I was standing over him offering a hand to get him back on his feet. I have no recollection of that.

The local police were called and both parties gave the authorities our version of what had transpired. The man did not deny initiating the attack nor did his wife deny following me into the bathroom. I had not suffered any injuries and saw no reason to press charges. I too would be upset if my wife was trailing a cable TV host around like a lost puppy. In a strange way, I admired the courage it took for him to open the bathroom door. It's the same courage I wish I'd shown back when the bar owner was holding my two hundred dollars hostage. The way I saw it, that couple would have enough problems to deal with once they got home.

What keeps life invigorating is the unexpected. Not knowing what is around the next turn keeps us in a constant state of wonder. It requires us to maintain the highest levels of alertness. Today's marketplace is a perfect example of survival of the fittest. We need to be smart, sharp, and savvy to obtain the things that bring us the greatest pleasure. By refusing to allow anything or anyone to dictate the direction of our lives, we're able to harness the power that I write about in my book, *The Choice Is Yours: 6 Keys to Putting Your Best into Action*. We all have that power. It is our birthright. The world around us and the people we let into our inner circle are what either enhance that power or blind us to its unlimited potential. Put on your best pair of boots and never stop kicking down the doors that lead to a better tomorrow.

CHAPTER 6

That's My Boy

Courage can come from a number of different sources. Some researchers say it is derived from life experiences while others claim it is simply ingrained deep within our DNA. Is bravery a result of nature or nurture? Surprisingly, it's relevance to both survival and success has often been stripped down and defined as little more than a knee-jerk reaction to a crisis.

I believe something altogether different. I am of the school that courage is instinctual and appears when we need it to the most. Our brain informs the body when it recognizes a need to jump into action and, as a result, we find the strength necessary to make us go where we didn't believe we could go. We see, perhaps on a previously undiscovered level, that what lies on the other side of whatever hurdle we may be facing is worth any pain or struggle that may be required to achieve it. To quote Nike's worldwide phenomena of a company slogan, we "Just Do It."

The word courage comes from the French word *Coeur*, meaning heart. I won't go into the importance of pouring your heart into your dreams because I devote an entire chapter to the subject in my widely successful personal development book, *The Choice Is Yours: Six Keys To Putting Your Best Into Action*. If you've never been to one of my live keynote presentations or have yet to read the book, I encourage you to invest the time to do both. The message you'll find within the pages has inspired tens of thousands of people just like you to kick their lives into motion and tackle each day with a full-speed-ahead mentality. It's a straightforward strategy that I have lived by for years and found to be a game changer.

I also believe that courage can be prominent where and when experience may be absent. Children are born fearless until society trains them to proceed with caution. Very little scares a child until an adult steps in and alerts them to dangers that may lie ahead. "Don't touch that stove!" "Get away from that snake!" I'm just as guilty of it as the next person. My children have endured more warnings to wear their bicycle helmets than any other kids we know. Though our intentions are good, it is our responsibility to protect our little ones. Is it possible, though, that through our own skepticism we are molding these brave, young minds only to see the bad in a situation? Imagine if our kids grew up to be adults who only saw the rewards and were blind to the risks.

In 2008, my ex-wife and I decided to move both households to the east coast from California. Thankfully, changes to the world of hosting have granted me the luxury of residing anywhere I please. As a result, I no longer felt tied to living in Los Angeles. Sure, the mountains and the oceans are beautiful and leaving the entertainment capital of the world may have been risky, but the traffic on the 405 was something I was not sad to see growing smaller in my rear view mirror. L.A. had given me all I needed from her. As parents we agreed that with its overcrowded schools, smog, and failing economy, California did not hold the bright future we wanted for our little ones. It is a town where dreams come true, I am a testament to that. It also can feel very transient at times and once you get the itch to move on with your life's journey there is only one way to scratch it. You need to pack your bags and welcome the adventure that lies ahead.

For the most part, Silver and I get along better than any formerly wedded couple we know. We operated well as a team, but the concept of "til death do us part" wasn't something either of us felt was anything to look forward to. Our home began to feel more like a well-run corporation than a romantic relationship, and we were wise enough to step back and think about the big picture. We both wanted our children to grow up with two parents who get along with each other, respect each other, and are able to naturally enjoy being in each other's company. It saddens me that so many kids are exposed to the problems of their parents. It is not only unfair to the children to have to carry those burdens, but it is also selfish of the parents.

Every marriage begins with the honeymoon phase and ours was no exception. The first few months were blissful, passionate, and exciting. It's not until real life sets in that people begin to see what a matrimony really is. It is, at its core, a partnership. And that partnership must be rock solid to endure the financial responsibilities, family issues, and work concerns that inevitably arise. For many couples, to deal with the cards life deals out, they put what was once important to them and their relationship on the shelf. Deep conversation, acts of respect and appreciation, and even sex begin to drift away only to be replaced by anger, frustration, and lame excuses meant to justify the shift. Suddenly, the once happy couple struggles to recall the bliss and finds themselves shrouded in bitterness. Fortunately for Silver and I, we had the wherewithal to realize that we were standing at a crossroads and made the decision we felt was best not just for us as individuals, but for the entire family.

No divorce is easy. The government has succeeded in turning marriage into a complex legal document binding two people together. Somewhere along the line it became necessary to enter into a contract situation, complete with dire financial penalties, to publicly showcase your commitment to someone. I'm astounded by how many young people continue to gamble their time, money, and future by rolling the dice on marriage. Playing a game with so much at risk and with the odds clearly stacked against you makes no sense. And agreeing to the forfeiture of half of one's assets should the arrangement not last until *death?* It reads as unrealistic to me. I am not stating in print that I will never marry again. I reserve the right to be blindsided by love at any given moment, but I do not feel the least bit incomplete without a ring on my finger. Should the right woman walk into my life, I can only hope that she too would see the wisdom of a prenuptial agreement. To me, it's as necessary and logical as wearing a seatbelt. Hopefully you never have to rely upon it saving you, but if you get sideswiped by an Escalade you're going to be glad you were wearing it.

All in all, Silver and I lucked out. Of course we have the occasional disagreement it's but never anything that cannot be worked out. I suppose we are not unlike the tourist in Vegas who can step away from the table after a winning hand. Sure, it was an expensive separation if you only look at it from a financial standpoint, but in the bigger scheme of things it was a win for everyone. My kids can have a nice dinner or spend holidays with both of their parents without tension or uneasiness, and I got to keep a good friend.

Our amicable divorce after seven years of marriage allowed us to step back and once again appreciate the qualities in that we initially found appealing in each other: she's an incredibly intelligent woman and the most devoted mother on Earth, and I am the most strikingly handsome man she's ever met. And because we share the common vision of raising our kids to be happy, healthy, and productive adults, neither of us could ask for anything more.

Timing is everything in show business and in life. Sometimes you find yourself in the right place at the right time, but you can also *place* yourself in the right place at the right time. Knowing when to hold 'em and when to fold 'em is crucial for success, and our timing with this move to the Boston area was ideal. The kids were young enough that they hadn't yet formed solid friendships they'd be heartbroken to leave behind. With the equity from the sale of the L.A. home that we purchased when we were married, Silver was able to afford a lovely property in a small New

England town that allowed her to be in a desirable school district. I found a charming little condominium in a sleepy little seaside village just a few miles away that allowed me enjoy life right on the beach. And my kids had both parents present and accounted for.

Escaping the overcrowding that plagues southern California was like a weight being lifted from all of our shoulders. Those of us who take full advantage of the benefits technology offers find that we can do more and more from wherever we happen to be. Meetings are now held via Skype and email. YouTube links effectively take the place of in-person auditions. Voiceover sessions are rarely conducted at an sound studio anymore, but rather in the artist's home workspace. And as long as I am in range of a major airport, I can be anywhere I need to be when I need to be there.

Like all parents, Silver and I wanted the best of the best for our children. Life in California was by no means miserable, but why settle for mediocrity when happiness lies just on the other side of a change? We both wanted the kids to be surrounded by a sense of community and to witness the changing of the seasons. Most of all, we wanted them to have access to the finest public education available and our new home(s) provided just that.

The school my children attended in the suburbs of Los Angeles was fine… just *fine*. The test scores were slightly above average and many parents in our area believed the private academy was the top of the education mountain. Perhaps it was, but just not the mountain I wanted to be at the peak of. The campus was tiny, the tuition was astronomical, and the children spent recess playing on hot blacktop without a blade of grass in sight. We knew there had to be something better and, to Silver's credit, she went out and found it.

We decided to make our move out east during the holiday break from school. The kids would complete the first semester in California and begin their new academic life in Massachusetts after Christmas. My daughter was still in preschool so she was completely indifferent. My son, however, was in third grade and the transition from a small private campus to a brand new, state-of-the-art public school bustling with thousands of students, many of them older than he, would be quite an adjustment.

I am extremely proud of the young man my son has become. I realize that most fathers hold their boys in high regard, but mine is everything I hope I was at his age. He is sensitive, a hard worker, responsible, honest, and intelligent. His instincts will take him far in life if he continues to make good decisions. That is something I preach incessantly to my children: make the right decision knowing that each choice comes with consequence and responsibility. As stated before, we all have that inner voice that points us in the right direction. The only time we get in trouble is when we intentionally ignore it.

When both of my children are passionate about something, they sink their teeth into it and will not loosen the grip until they have mastered it. This is true of everything from martial arts to ice skating and from horseback riding to fishing. They never shy away from a challenge and I've yet to see one of them step down when the going gets tough. I no longer worry about how they will handle changes, but the move east occurred when Mason was just eight years old.

Children have an invincibility that is unmatched by any adult. I've encountered some powerful characters in my life, but kids dream big and they fear nothing. Sadly, life often dulls the shine of youthful bravery. As we grow older, we take our share of hits and the majority of people often choose the safer route if it means avoiding further disappointment, rejection, or pain. The young have yet to experience life's setbacks and, therefore, can attack each day with the fearless abandon. This is to be encouraged and supported which is why my children and I created The Newton Fund 4 Kids in 2014.

Through the generous donations of our contributors, NF4K is able to assist children's hospitals across the United States by funding state-of-the-art pediatric healthcare to any child that needs it. When a child is sick or injured, the last thing a family should worry about is how they will meet the financial obligations associated with the treatment. Facilities like Cardinal Glennon Medical Center in my hometown of St. Louis, MO, eliminates that unease. We are a proud part of a much larger machine that provides private rooms for all patients, Level 1 trauma centers, and a comprehensive fetal care institute which offers surgical interventions to help babies before birth. The lives being touched are countless. The work being done is miraculous. In addition to the much-needed treatments, we are showing these children through love and action that the world values them. They are our tomorrow. We're also showing their families that they are not alone.

    I woke up long before I needed to on what would be Mason's first day at his new school. It wasn't ambition that forced me out of bed; it was nerves. For a man who thrives on being in front of thousands of people for a living, the queasiness in my stomach was something I was not accustomed to. My biggest concern was that Mason might be feeling the same anxiety that I was feeling. After all, this was a monumental day in his young life. A day in which he would face the stares and scrutiny of a classroom filled with strange faces. To my knowledge, he had never been so exposed and vulnerable. Had he absorbed enough self-confidence and strength from observing Silver and me? Perhaps he had been preparing himself for this day in ways known only to him. Or maybe, just maybe, he was actually looking forward to the new path his life was about to take. It takes wisdom to see the silver lining that hides within a new beginning, and though I'm not a prayerful man, I asked out loud for my son to choose the path that would bring him the most happiness.

    The three of us had been given the opportunity to take a brief tour of the new school prior to the beginning of classes. We visited the library, the gymnasium, the cafeteria, even his classroom. Mason also met his new teacher, Mrs. Smith. Though he would not be walking in blindly, the building seemed vast even to me, and it would be a much different environment when filled with children returning from a break. Though surrounded by bedlam, my son seemed to be taking it all in stride. He was silent for the most part, only asking the occasional question and nodding as things were pointed out to him.

    After a quick shower, I made myself a cup of coffee and drove the short distance to Silver's house. We would go to school that morning as a family. Mason would know that he was supported and loved, but he would also know that once he walked through those doors, it was his responsibility to make the very best of the situation.

The Host With The Most

The three of us checked in at the main office. He sat silently and absorbed his new surroundings. Silver and I were the anxious ones. Before his new teacher arrived to escort him to class, I took him aside and knelt down beside him. There was so much fatherly advice whirling around in my head and I wanted to share it all with him but there wasn't time. I narrowed all of my thoughts down to one piece of wisdom my own father had shared with me so many times over the years: "Just be yourself."

I wanted to tell him to be nice to others and they (hopefully) will be nice to you. I wanted to beg him to make healthy choices at lunch and pay attention to the teacher. I wanted to instruct him to be on his best behavior and to learn all he could possibly learn. Telling him just to be who he is seemed to encapsulate all of that. He knows who and what he is. I've seen the power of his smile and the impact his personality has on myself and others. I felt confident that if he went in just being the kid he is, everything would play out fine.

As parents, we sometimes feel as if our kids just nod in agreement with what we are saying in order to appease us. It seems our words go in one ear and right out the other, but on this day I could see the words resonating with Mason. He gave me a nod that said, "Don't worry Mom and Dad, I'm going to be just fine."

With a kiss and a hug from both of his parents, my young son turned and walked confidently down the hallway with his new teacher, never once looking back.

Silver and I stood together and watched with parental pride and wonder. My nerves were washed away and replaced with the confidence of knowing that we were raising one heck of a kid. Tears were streaming down both of our faces as we looked at each other and made our way out to the parking lot.

Our family would experience a similar transition many years later. The New England winters got the best of us by 2015 and we once again packed up both domains and headed back west. The desert would now be home and with it would come new experiences, new friends, and new schools. My kids were obviously a little older and better equipped for change. We prepared for it by taking several trips to the new area which allowed all of us to familiarize ourselves with our new surroundings. Nothing, however, can fully prepare a child for a new school. But they did it again. Both of them approached their first days with optimism, if not a sense of adventure.

If a child can see the wonder beyond the fear, why can't an adult? Why must change be terrifying? Why the hesitation to explore the unknown? What a gift it is to live with avidity rather than trepidation. There are certainly those who have mastered the art of taking no prisoners and turning obstacles into opportunity, and I hope you are among them. But shouldn't we all live with such fervor? Pain is inevitable, but so are recovery and growth. Have our experiences not demonstrated this time after time? Dreams cost you nothing. An enormous dream requires the same amount of energy as a minute dream, so what is so frightening about going for the brass ring?

When you see someone you are attracted to why not approach that man or woman and introduce yourself? Place the potential outcomes on a mental scale and weigh out the risk vs. the reward. You'll see that you have absolutely nothing to lose and everything to gain. By approaching that individual, you are opening the door to endless possibility. By chickening out, you have guaranteed a lost opportunity. You know what will happen if you allow fear to make the decision for you… nothing! But having the guts to take the shot could literally change the rest of your life.

Because we have been trained to be afraid, or at the very least cautious, I cannot simply *tell* you to wake up tomorrow and be brave. You can't dismiss fear. The world is filled with mean and nasty people who are looking to take what belongs to you and chop you down to nothing. Rather than succumb to fear, I encourage you to challenge it. Show your fangs and face what terrifies you the most head on. Whether it is a new responsibility at work or a challenge that is deeply personal, I assure you it isn't anything you can't beat if you put forth the required effort. Life is too short to be afraid of taking a chance. Opportunities should never go unexplored and a certain level of apprehension can be healthy. But can you muster the strength to wave at reluctance in passing rather than allow it to make your decisions for you? As far as emotions go, I believe fear pales in comparison to joy, eagerness, and enthusiasm. The only control fear actually has over you is its ability to disarm and debilitate your chances of winning.

If you have not purchased and read *The Choice Is Yours: 6 Keys To Putting Your Best Into Action*, please do so right away. Keep a copy with you when you travel and by your bedside at night. Absorb the information before you fall asleep so it will soak into your subconscious and become a part of your thought process. It will strengthen you with the knowledge that you have the power to choose what your life will become. Don't be a sucker. Take control of a situation before the situation takes control of you and your fears will begin to vanish into thin air.

Live life like a child and see an open window not as something you should be afraid of falling out of, but as an opening to a world filled with beauty, challenges, and rewards.

CHAPTER 7

WHAT EBAY TAUGHT ME ABOUT LIFE

It was in pristine condition, if I may say so myself. That's not hyperbole. It was less than ninety days old without a scratch on it. I mean, I had really pampered this baby. After dropping my fair share face first onto unforgiving parking lot surfaces and into toilet bowls across the country, I knew that a used iPhone 5s like mine could easily fetch $175, maybe even $200, online. That's the kind of cash that would certainly cushion the early termination fee that AT&T had looming over my head.

    I do give the AT&T phone representative credit for using every objection rebuttal in her training manual in an effort to keep me as a customer. Her concern made me feel loved and appreciated like very few women in my life have. She quoted my average usage statistics as if she'd known me since childhood and even recommended alternative other plans in case cost was the issue. She did everything but offer to come to my house when she finished work and detail my car. Unfortunately for her, her efforts were in vain.

AT&T and I had run our course. The seven-year love affair had ended as abruptly as a dropped call. My heart now belonged to Verizon and, try as she might, the friendly voice on the other end of the line was not going to dissuade me from pursuing this new relationship. Men sacrifice many things in the name of love. The taxes and penalties meant nothing as I found myself blinded by the glow of unlimited talk and text, more data, and a brand new iPhone 6.

My upgrade, once complete, ended up feeling somewhat bittersweet. Yes, I had a shiny new smartphone with faster speed and a sharper camera, but seeing my former companion, the phone that had accompanied me across so many miles and captured so many memories, lifelessly staring at me from my kitchen counter saddened me. Though without a single bar of power remaining, the lifeless screen seemed to be saying, *"Was it me? Did I do something to hurt you?"* No my sweet outdated tech gadget, it's all me. I needed to move on. I'm sorry. I hope you'll soon find another who will appreciate you for all that you are.

At the time of this writing, it is estimated that over 100 million people use eBay to either sell items they no longer have a need for or to purchase items they do. The only thing easier than selling an item on eBay is making a buy. Within minutes, and from the comfort of your own home, consumers can accomplish what used to require hours of driving, parking, and mall trolling.

The Internet grants us access to most of the world. As scary and invasive as that may seem to some, that access could very well result in revenue for those who know how to tap into its potential. By uploading a few photos of my older model phone, a potential buyer in Zimbabwe can read the description and make an educated purchase, possibly finding exactly what she has been looking for at a price far below retail. I wasn't looking to retire off of what I made from my sale, I just wanted fair market value. I win. They win. eBay wins. That's the American (and Zimbabwean) way.

Much like a television or radio host must involve the audience in some way if the show is to be a hit, eBay does a nice job of making me feel as if

I'm part of the fold by sharing selling tips, incorporating a rating system, and keeping inventory of all of my past transactions. Although I'm fully aware that my nearly insignificant purchase and selling fees aren't paying the monthly heating bills at eBay's San Jose headquarters, it's always nice to know that your business is appreciated. Todd Newton may not matter much, but 100 million users with Internet access and the eBay app have created a commerce giant that has changed the shopping space forever.

I am grateful for my ten plus year relationship with the retail behemoth. eBay has not only provided an outlet on which to sell useless swag garnered from Hollywood award show gift bags, but it continuously saves me money on items such as car chargers, pet supplies, and even the many neckties that I often give to audience members during *TPIR Live* performances. Again, win-win-win. But the most revered takeaway is the series of valuable life lessons one learn as a result of the eBay experience.

We are *all* salespeople.

In life, as in business, every one of us is in sales. We market ourselves to friends, business associates, clients and potential romantic partners through the words we choose, the way we dress, and even the photos we select to serve as our social media profile pictures. In today's sound bite society, first impressions are made in a matter of seconds and image *is* everything. Remember, you are the product.

eBay rewards those who show a shrewd sales technique. When posting an item for sale, it is left solely to the seller to creatively (yet accurately) describe the item they have to offer. Keeping in mind that the buyer does not have the luxury of touching the potential purchase as they would at a mall, we must demonstrate the item's value using only our words and a collection of thumbnail photos.

The posted headline must be eye-catching and intrigue buyers enough to want to click on that item rather than a handful of other postings of comparable items (our competition). Can we not say the same for our professional profiles? When I scan the web to see who is out there hosting what, I am often taken aback by the fluff and pandering I come across in hosting bios. Inaccuracies and exaggerations seem to run wild. By being economical with the truth you are only doing a disservice to yourself.

You may fool the rookies, but the experienced online shopper will see right through it. Rather than coming up with words to enhance its appeal, search for ways to enhance its value.

I recently read Jeffrey Gitomer's incredible book, *The Little Red Book of Selling*. What an informative and inspirational read. Though I do not earn my living pushing vacuum cleaners door to door, I found the tips within the pages to be of enormous value to me as The Host with the Most® as well as with Newton Luxury Realty. Whether I am on camera or negotiating the sale of a beautiful home in Scottsdale, AZ, no one will work harder to market my particular brand than yours truly. I am selling myself every day, not only as a host and as The Celebrity Real Estate Agent™, but also as an author and keynote speaker. The sales techniques that Jeffrey put forth in his book add to the power of my overall presentation.

One area of the book that I found particularly interesting was the author's interview with an Atlanta-based salesperson, Terri Norris. For over three years running, Terri has been Cintas' number one salesperson. Jeffrey asked Terri what she believed her ten best qualities were. Her answers painted a clear picture as to why she is the best of the best. Included in her list were concentrating on the details and possessing an unspoken integrity.

Integrity is not only one of my favorite qualities in a person, it's also one of my favorite words. In fact, I have it tattooed on my left arm. Having integrity is a fundamental element of achievement. Just as it is crucial to be honest and upfront in the description of items you sell on eBay (and punishable if you aren't), so is it vital in the offering of your talents to the world. Integrity is not the way others perceive you, it's how you perceive yourself when others aren't around. It's pride in one's self and a clear conscience. It's doing what's right simply because it's right, not because of Karma or the fear of retribution.

If a seller is fraudulent in the presentation of an item sold on eBay they run the risk of a negative review, forfeiting the money from the sale, or possibly even having their account deactivated. In life, the effects of being deceitful are even more damning. The risk of losing a job, a criminal record, or irreversible damage to a reputation are just a few of the very real possibilities.

In life as on eBay, one must be upfront and honest in the marketing of the product you wish to share with the world: *you*.

Money *can* buy happiness.

Close your eyes and envision three things that bring you pure joy. Do not feel as if you need to get all sappy and sentimental. Just focus on the first three images that pop into your unfiltered mind. There are no right or wrong answers here and if you feel a bit greedy your secret will be safe with me.

If you are at all human, your triad of happy things included at least one material item (probably more). A new car, a big house with an infinity pool and home theater, or even a new wardrobe are the norm. Greed and excess are components of how the human brain operates. We are conditioned to want bigger, brighter, and better. These are the traditional signs of success and achievement. But being human also means that you have a soul which instructed you to push that image of a 70" flat screen television out of the way and replace it with world peace or clean water for all. If you thought about it for more than two seconds, your conscious mind most likely reminded you that providing nutritious food and shelter for your family was more important than that vacation in Fiji you've been dreaming of.

The point of this exercise in personal awareness is not to shame you into point you toward making the humane choice or make you feel guilty for the items you imagined. You shouldn't be remorseful for wanting more. You work hard and what you wear, drive, and eat are tangible markers of your status in society. Possessions serve as reminders of how far we've come and motivate us to keep on going in order to grab the latest model or the newest fashion. There's nothing wrong with that. The point I want to make is that the best things in life *are not free*.

Wait a minute, Todd. All my life people have been telling me the exact opposite. Why should I believe you?

You should believe me because it's the truth. And I'm going to prove it to you.

Does knowing that your family members are in good health make you happy? Of course it does. As a matter of fact, it's at the very top of my personal list. But when my daughter recently fractured her little ankle, it didn't heal itself. I couldn't simply snap my fingers and turn paper towels into X-rays. Her crutches weren't constructed out of tree branches. Quality care comes with a hefty price tag. That is actually you'll find at the core of my charity, Newton Fund 4 Kids. No child should be denied treatment or only have access to mediocre healthcare because of a family's inability to pay. Whether it's nutritious food, clean water, or medicine, keeping your family healthy requires opening your wallet.

Let's look at another example. Have you ever taken a "me day" and just gone to the park or to the beach to read a good book? Of course you have. I love taking a stroll by the water early in the morning. It's when I achieve my most peaceful and productive state. I can silently plan out my day as I gaze out at the waves gently rolling onto the shore. Those beaches and parks are a great escape and they don't cost anything to visit, right? Wrong.

That park in which you run, walk your dog, and watch your kids play is maintained by you, the taxpayer. A portion of that chunk Uncle Sam takes out of your paycheck each week pays to keep the grass cut in the summer and the sidewalk clear of snow in the winter. Not to mention the fact that you wouldn't even be able to read this book if it weren't for our country's tax-funded school systems. This doesn't mean you should enjoy these amenities any less. We're fortunate as Americans to have access to such luxuries. If anything, you should find it more rewarding knowing that you're helping to foot the bill.

The average American spends money from the moment we open our eyes in the morning until we crawl into bed at night. But the spending doesn't necessarily end when you turn out the lights. All the more reason to work harder and be better than most see as logical. Some foolishly believe that there is no expense in simply closing our eyes in search of peaceful slumber. Dreamland couldn't possibly have a cover charge, could it? Wake up! Think about what goes into a good sleep. A fluffy pillow. A nice mattress. Your favorite blanket. A glass of water on the nightstand. Heat in the winter and air conditioning in the summer. Your pajamas. The cash register never stops ringing which is why you can never stop improving on your brand and carving out your niche.

Make no mistake about it; *money makes the world go around*. I've just proven that with the most basic of examples. Love is the most beautiful emotion a person can experience, but how will we ever find someone to fall in love with if we never go anywhere or experience anything? Museums, coffee shops, online dating sites all charge admission and even offer automated payment options to make it easier to spend your money. Laughter is the best medicine, but we find it alongside good company (and often good wine). Charity, peace, and goodwill all make our planet a more glorious place but the exchange of currency, in one form or another, is always required.

eBay is a convenient reminder that it is perfectly fine to expect money in exchange for the items I no longer have a use for. One man's trash is another man's treasure. Whether it be coins or chickens, the monetary exchange has been the way in which a person accumulates something that brings him comfort or pleasure since as early as 9000 BC. The same philosophy applies to what you choose to do for a living. Promoting your value is paramount because there is no guarantee that there will be a demand for what you are selling.

When you choose your life's path, it is wise to study the course history and determine if your vocation provides a needed service or offers a solution to a problem. The demand will determine your value. Your value is your worth. Your dreams alone are worth nothing unless they lead to something that is of value to you or to others. Making money *will* bring you happiness if you focus on a career that you enjoy pouring your heart and soul into. I write these words from experience. Never once have I felt as if I was going to "work." Remember, I don't *have* to, I *get* to. You should *get* to, too.

Now close your eyes and again visualize the three things in life that are most important to you. Accept that they cost money but embrace the fact that you work hard in an effort to obtain them. You deserve them. Focus not on the price tag but on the way these things make you feel as a person and a provider. That's not selfishness, it's satisfaction. And without satisfaction, the world would be a very empty place.

It's all about the follow through.

Services rendered. Pay the man.

I've repeated JR's words to myself more times than I can remember. The quote is not only applicable to a deal made on eBay, but it's a good life lesson. First comes the work, then comes the reward. Don't spend it if you don't have it. Being a person of your word and following through on what you say you will do sets you apart from the rest. Being reliable and responsible are qualities that may be scarce, but are always present in great achievers. It's all a matter of envisioning the bigger picture and thinking ahead.

My kids like to jokingly point out that I am never late for anything. This is true. I believe that if you are right on time, you are five minutes late. This stems from my disdain for being kept waiting. Many times in life, the bird that gets the worm is the one that got their early. And the things that come to those who wait are what those of us who got there first refer to as table scraps. Being where you said you'd be and doing what you committed to do are just part of the follow through.

Think of the classic *Seinfeld* episode in which Jerry goes to the car rental counter to retrieve his vehicle only to find that they are all out of cars. Jerry explains to the attendant that anyone can *take* a reservation but the important thing is *holding* the reservation. Sadly, the comedy here comes from reality as we all have been disappointed by an individual or business who did not live up to a promise. As a result, we are reluctant to take that person or service at their word in the future.

When my son made his first sale on eBay, he was ecstatic. I was so proud of the way he took the time to accurately describe the item. The selected photos were clear and revealing. His overall command of the site was impressive and I will never forget his smile when the money from the sale appeared in his bank account. He had been bitten by the entrepreneurial bug and was now officially on his way to becoming a mover and shaker.

No deal is complete without the safe and timely delivery of the product. No payment shall be made until services are rendered, right? Mason understood that the final step was packing and shipping his item in a prompt manner. The payout was not officially his until that item arrived at the buyer's address. But, as a result of his efficiency and attention to every detail of the transaction, he ultimately received his first positive rating.

Life lessons are all around us if we continuously scratch to see what lies just below the surface. By removing a layer or two of what we accept as reality, we often uncover a clear and refreshing truth. I'm aware that eBay is just one of a countless number of websites used by millions of people each day. As previously mentioned, I've been a user myself for a decade and only now have I come to the realizations shared in this chapter. Maybe it's age or maybe it's the fact that I woke up at four o'clock this morning and found myself in need of a new iPhone case. Either way, the truth is the truth. Life and curiosity have ways of teaching you the lessons you won't find in textbooks.

CHAPTER 8

TATTOOED IN HELL

"Just one. It begins on this wrist, continues up and across my chest, and ends at the base of my other wrist. Just one big, lovable hunk of painted flesh."

That's my standard response when asked how many tattoos I have. Obviously I am being flippant. I've accumulated many tattoos over the years and no two are linearly connected. And other than those devoted to my family, few are even related in meaning. Those in the tattoo world refer to my pattern of collecting as the "postage stamp" style. I am a collector. During my travels I locate a shop, seek out an artist I connect with, and have him/her place a piece on me. When I look at my chest in the mirror each morning or catch a glimpse of my arms throughout the day, I can always remember where I was when I had it placed. Some people buy postcards and t-shirts. I prefer to carry my art with me. Since the first question I am usually asked is how many pieces adorn my body, I keep it simple. One. It has a friendly ring to it and is normally met with a look of genuine surprise.

There are many misconceptions when it comes to body art; whether it be tattoos, piercings, or even hairstyles. Contrary to popular belief, a tattoo is not always meant to relay a deep message or belief. Many of mine do happen to have a certain degree of meaning. For example, the clock on my right elbow is set to the time of day my son was born. The microphone on my arm represents a lifelong dream of becoming a broadcaster. My ex-wife's zodiac sign on my left shoulder represents the eternal bond of parenthood that holds us together. The Parkinson's disease awareness flower on my left arm is a tribute to the courage with which my father faces the disease on a daily basis. But because I have an owl permanently etched into my right forearm does not indicate that I travel through this life seeking wisdom any more than it means I really enjoy a Tootsie Pop.

Aside from those mentioned, the majority of the colors, designs, and words that I have chosen to place on the canvas that is my body have been so placed simply because I liked the way they looked at the time. I love both the traditional Sailor Jerry-style of tattoo art that is present in the anchor on my chest, the pin-up cowgirl under a banner that reads "Livin' the Dream" on my back, and the two swallows on my right arm (the blue for my son and the pink for my daughter). Sailors of old received similar swallow art to symbolize a safe return home after a long journey. Believe me, as much as I love traveling and hosting for you, there is nothing more rejuvenating and rewarding than returning home.

I also have a deep appreciation for Japanese art. This is evident by the work covering my left arm and chest. Artists such as the legendary Ozuma-sensei, Horiyoshi 3, and even the more recent commercial sensation, Ed Hardy, decorate the human body with wind bars, koi, and water using both vibrant color and masterful shading. The human eye naturally absorbs it. To me, there is nothing more aesthetically pleasing than the fine line work and rich coloring of a new tattoo.

Other forms of artistic expression, whether it be music, painting, poetry, or sculpture, are often created for the pleasure and commercial appeal of those observing it, whereas an individual's tattoo is not for anyone other than themselves. Though often in plain view, a tattoo's relevance, if one exists at all, is inherently private. Body art does not define the person, but it often describes them.

One does not accumulate as many tattoos as I have overnight. Each piece is a process. A design needs to resonate with you. You need to imagine it somewhere on your person. You need to collaborate with your artist. She or he needs to draw it up until it speaks to you. Then, when you are satisfied with the design, you go under the needle. The popular tattoo reality shows that we see on television give the false impression that a full arm piece can be completed in thirty minutes. Any artist will tell you that nothing could be further from the truth. A tattoo is a commitment, an investment of both time and money. For me, it is also a form of therapy as I often find tattoo parlors to be bustling with people who are not afraid to remove the filters and tell it like it is.

I have visited every state in this country of ours and the pages of my passport are filled with the stamps of lands far away that have opened their borders for me. I've taken my share of pictures and spent plenty of cash on souvenirs that end up getting tossed into the trash, but the real journal of my travels can be explored through the tattoos on my arms, chest, and back. Yes, I can look at any tattoo on my body and tell you where I got it, who the artist was, and in many instances, the music that was blaring as my skin was being transformed.

Sitting for a tattoo is a unique experience involving its own sights, sounds, and smells. Each of which can instantly take you to another time and place. Whether we're talking about the roses I had placed on my shoulder in Chicago, the shark with a flower in his mouth that I got in Nashville, or the Japanese kanji symbol for fatherhood that I received from Angelina Jolie's artist in a Tokyo hotel room, my ink is the map of my personal journey. It is like no other map in the world. When it comes to one-of-a-kind, you can keep your snowflakes. I'll take a tattoo.

Hot Rod Tattoo in Atlantic City, NJ, was exactly what one envisions when thinking of a New Jersey tattoo parlor. Located across the street from a low-rent strip joint and down the block from a casino that was years past its heyday, the shop was so stereotypical that it could've come straight off of a movie set. The death metal music was too loud. The walls were cluttered with flash art samples of butterflies, daggers, and skulls. And the artists were covered head to toe in faded blue prison art. All in all, it was the perfect place to de-flower myself and get my first tattoo.

I've since come to better appreciate the relationship between an artist and a client. *Wisdom* gained from *Age* has taught me that if I am going to spend a few hours and a few hundred bucks with someone, then we better have something to talk about. Today's tattoo artist often finds himself in the same role your local bartender or your grandmother's hairstylist once filled. They become armchair therapists and sounding blocks. They become the ideal listener because they often will be one of those rare individuals who tell you what they really think about love, politics, or art without any concern for repercussions. Plus, they are a captive audience. They have nowhere else to be than right there with you. Tattoo therapy is the only kind of therapy I need.

The Old Market in Omaha, Nebraska, is the city's most historic and eclectic neighborhood. The cobblestone streets are lined with quaint shops, restaurants, every type of bar, and art galleries. When night falls, the sounds of horse-drawn carriages and live music rise into the Midwestern sky. It was a wonderful place for my close friend Amanda and I to spend a night off during the 2013 tour.

Amanda is the baby sister I never had. We began working and traveling together when she was just nineteen years old and have involuntarily and unintentionally shared some of our most interesting road experiences together. She is one of those special friends that can read my mind well enough to order for me at a restaurant, and I am the protector that allows her parents to sleep soundly at night knowing that their only daughter is in good hands. But what I adore most about Amanda is the fact that she never balks when I drag her all over a new town in search of a tattoo shop.

"I'm looking to get a lucky horseshoe," I explained as the navigational app on my smartphone led us down yet another empty block. "The shop has to be around here somewhere. I promise it will be a quick piece to do."

Sure enough, the shop was close by. But it was also closed. The website had apparently not been updated and Amanda and I had ventured more than two miles since leaving our hotel only to find the lights out and the doors locked.

"You're lucky I've good walking shoes on. Otherwise you'd be on your own, Mister" was Amanda's only response. I was fully aware that the term 'Mister' was reserved for those moments in which she was frustrated with me. I knew I was monopolizing her time and being greedy with her patience, so I hailed the first taxi we saw and instructed the driver to take us back to where we were staying.

The thing about a tattoo is that once a particular piece has infiltrated your thoughts, it is virtually impossible to eliminate it from your mind. It seems to be present even in sleep. My ex-wife used to say that if she sees a pair of shoes or an outfit she really likes, she immediately walks away. If she is still thinking about it a couple of days later, she knows it's a sound purchase. The same can be said about a tattoo. The crown I have on my upper back had been fermenting in the recesses of my brain for weeks. It held no meaning to me, I just liked the way it looked on skin. My vision was to customize it by adding some shading and coloring the decorative jewels with the tones of my kids' birthstones. It looked magnificent in my mind and translated beautifully when I had it done late one in a shop near the Seattle Fish Market.

Why I had a hankering for a traditional horseshoe tattoo in Omaha I do not know. It is, after all , widely viewed as a symbol for luck and that is not something I believe in. I suppose it may have something to do with the fact that it is a popular traditional piece and there are countless variations of how it may be applied. There is no one right size or color combination. It can be placed anywhere on the body and blends well with future or existing pieces. All I can tell you is that I had to have that damn horseshoe and I had one night to get it done before our show at the Orpheum Theater. After the performance would be too late as it we'd be wheels up and onward to the next city.

Amanda and I enjoyed an extraordinary dinner at a small, family-owned Italian restaurant a few blocks from our hotel. Not wanting to risk wasting her time the way I did earlier in the day, I said goodbye and took one final stroll into the Old Market to pick up some souvenirs for my kids. It was a beautiful night for an after dinner walk and coincidentally I came across two tattoo shops that leaned toward the trendy side. Unfortunately, hip isn't really my style when it comes to tattoo parlors. I like a little grit and grime. I prefer the artist working on me to *look* like a tattoo artist and not a model from Abercrombie & Fitch.

It's been my experience that if you dare to venture just outside of the busier shopping districts, you just may stumble upon a fascinating and unexpected subculture. My grandmother would refer to these areas as "the types of neighborhoods you roll up your windows and lock your doors" when driving through. She was probably right. Pawn shops become commonplace. Thrift stores replace the franchise superstores. Check cashing outlets attempt to lure you in by promising advances of up to $200 interest-free. And the neon glow of a tattoo parlor that stays open just a little later than the competition awaits just around the next corner.

There were no flashing signs or valet parking attendants like at the more mainstream shops across town. The simplicity of the word TATTOO painted on the door in blood red lettering said what needed to be said. If you wanted ink you could get it here, but don't expect any frills. Peering through the foggy storefront window, the only indication of life I could see inside was a giant fish tank. Expensive backlighting made the slow, calculated swimming patterns of the fish seem almost mysterious. This was going to be the place.

I was surprised to find the door unlocked. Part of me expected the shop to be closed for the night, if not permanently out of business. Any traffic this place saw had to come from word of mouth. Yelp reviews be damned. The artists that chose to set up shop here no doubt had a legion of loyal customers if they were able keep the lights on in such an undesirable location, not to mention maintaining the costs of that tank. If anyone was inside, I was sure they would be working on another customer and may not take too kindly to being interrupted.

"Over here," I heard a voice say as the man behind came rolling out on a stool from a corner drawing station.

"Jesus, you scared the hell out of me," no cool in my voice whatsoever. "I didn't see anyone in here."

He was dressed all in black. T-shirt, jeans, and motorcycle boots. His arms were covered in ink. His jawline painted with scruff. Pencils tucked behind both ears. One would think he was trying a little too hard to achieve this look if it didn't come off so effortlessly. A distressed bomber jacket the same style as his footwear hung from a chipped antique hat rack in the shadowed corner by the door.

"What can I help you with?" Clearly he wasn't in the mood for a late night chat with a game show host, so I cut right to the chase. These first few minutes in a tattoo shop are make or break for me. I've met some artists who are incredibly accommodating and will go to great lengths to put something on your body that you'll be proud of for the rest of your life. I've also encountered those who display an err of false nobility. They treat the client as if it is a privilege to be in their presence. I never give that type of artist a dime because ultimately they do not care about the finished product. They want you in and out so the next chump can plop down in their chair. That's not my style. I refuse to taint my love for the tattoo experience by giving these types of artists my business. Tattooing is like any business in that there's always another shop right down the street offering something similar. But, on this particular Omaha evening, my options appeared to be very limited and his gruffness appealed to my sense of adventure. I told him about the horseshoe that had been in my dreams as of late and asked if he might be able to take me in before closing shop.

"Sure, man. We can do that. What colors did you have in mind?" It's always a good sign when the artist asks for your ideas right away. It's also always a good idea to provide that artist a degree of creative freedom, especially with something as basic as a horseshoe. Often he or she see things in their mind's eye that you do not. An added line or some extra shading to add dimension can enhance a piece beyond your wildest imagination. He was the artist and I was giving him room to create.

"Let's go bright," I said. "Red, yellow, orange. Whatever you're picturing." Sometimes you need to let go and allow the artist's creativity to shine. Walking into a shop with a photo you pulled off of Instagram defeats the purpose of a tattoo. The tattoo in that photo is already on someone else. Why would you want it on yourself? Considering that very few of my pieces are from the same artist, it adds character and individuality to my collection. In fact, I requested that he draw the design freehand so it would not be identical to any other horseshoe I'd ever seen or that he'd ever done.

Judging by the subtle nod of his head, I could tell he enjoyed having the shackles removed. He knew I wasn't some tattoo virgin who wandered in off the street with twenty bucks in my pocket hoping for a deal. I believe he now saw me as someone who respected the craft, possibly even as much as he did. He rolled back over to his drawing table and grabbed a handful of Sharpies; one red, one orange, and one green. Without a word, he began sketching directly onto my skin.

His strokes were fleeting and undefined, but the artist in him was locked onto a vision only he could see. He never even took the time to tell me his name before getting down to business, but he most definitely invested the time in his art. What he was creating would serve as an extension of himself. This tattoo would be permanent and, in a sense, serve as a mobile billboard showcasing his passion.

Finally, after the inside of my right arm began to look like a dry erase board in an elementary school classroom, he scribbled a few finishing touches on the rough outline and snapped each colored cap back onto its respective maker. Without no verbal indication that he was finished, he turned away from me and began to arrange his equipment.

I've been tattooed enough to know that when the artist begins unwrapping the single-use needles and covering the area with paper towels, the action is about to get underway. Gone are the tattoo parlors of old where the same needle is used for victim after victim until it becomes too dull and torturous to do the job. Today's tattoo shop resembles a dermatologist's office. Say what you will about a tattoo artist who is covered head to toe in ink, at least he wears rubber gloves when he works and his office is sanitized multiple times throughout the day and night. Sometimes as I drift off to sleep at night, I think back to the many hands I shook and the strangers I kissed during that day's taping or that evening's show and realize that I forgot to wash my hands before I went to bed. Needless to say, his approach to cleanliness was greatly appreciated and admired.

Arms are a painless safe haven when it comes to getting a tattoo. That is until you begin venturing up near the armpit. That's where the sting kicks in. Ribs, however, are a different story. Earlier in that same *TPIR Live* tour we'd had a day off in the great city of Austin, TX. Austin has always been one of my favorite towns. I love the authentic BBQ, the live music that can be found at any hour up and down Sixth Street, and, of course, the beautiful Texas ladies. A friend of mine had turned me on to an artist named Chris who specialized in the Sailor Jerry pin-up girl tattoos. I'd always yearned for a pin-up piece but had never had the time to sit for one.

I love the traditional display of Americana a pin-up radiates and reached out to Chris to see if he could find time in his schedule to color me up with something special while I was in town. A good tattoo artist is often booked well in advance, and they never do their clients or themselves the disservice of overbooking. An artist does not like to feel rushed and booking clients back to back creates undo pressure resulting in a less than perfect piece. But after hearing that I was a friend of a friend, Chris kindly agreed to come in on his day off to work on me. I'm sure knowing his work would be on a TV guy who gets featured in tattoo trade magazines from time to time played a bit of a part in his willingness to forfeit his free time, but I was willing to cash in on any and all favors.

After locking down the appointment, I immediately went to work designing the ladies I wanted to have placed on each rib cage. On my left side would be a lovely blonde in an evening dress. She would be both classy and sassy with just enough thigh exposed through the slit in her gown to reveal a small heart tattoo with a T in it.

On my right side would be a brunette cowgirl wearing a feisty grin and boots. She too would sport a heart tattoo with my initial. Both ladies would be unique to me and something I wouldn't be ashamed to have my children see. No nudity. No overtly sexual vibe. Just old school ink done right in Texas. I couldn't think of a better way to spend an afternoon.

Until Chris' needle touched the thin skin covering my ribcage.

"Dude, you're going to have to hold still for me," Chris said. "I'm doing the outline and you want her to be perfect." We flipped a coin to decide which piece we'd tackle first. When the quarter landed on the hardwood floor of the shop and showed tails, Chris taped the stencil of the blonde on my left side and we were off to the races. But within five seconds I had already made up my mind that there was no way in hell we'd be doing the other side too. My friends Jay and Stevie had accompanied me to the shop, both looking to get their first tattoos, but soon decided they'd rather day drink at the bar across the street than endure one minute more of my fidgeting and screaming.

Each second seemed like an hour. I'd never felt anything like it before. I had been tattooed on my arms, back, chest, and feet but apparently had not done my due diligence when it came to the ribs. Chris explained that there was no muscle little fat in that area. Nothing to absorb the needle like on an arm. It's just skin to bone.

What choice did I have? Chris had already started the piece. He couldn't stop now or I'd be left with nothing but random black lines amounting to nothing. Not that I've been seen once with my shirt off since the *Wild On* days on E!, but that didn't matter. I really wanted these pin-up girls. In fact, I was looking forward to them more than any other piece I'd ever gotten, but the pain was excruciating. All I could do was man up and battle through it.

We did agree, however, that we were not going to attempt the other rib. Chris and I both came to the conclusion, in light of current circumstances, that the cowgirl should go on my back. At least that would cut my agony in half. And with that little bit of solace, I was able to put on a brave face and trudge on.

What would have normally only taken two hours ended up taking more than four. Stevie and Jay giggled drunkenly as the pain forced me to call time out every twenty minutes or so. I was miserable and taking these breaks to check the progress only seemed to make things harder. Chris was a perfectionist, and my agony was secondary to his vision.

When the piece was finally finished, I must say that was thrilled with the outcome. Chris' work was everything I heard it would be and more.

Each lady stands close to nine inches tall and the detail is exceptional. I wouldn't put myself through that again, that part of my body is now off limits, but I love what I see in the mirror each morning. Yes, Austin not only has a special place in my heart but also on my ribs.

In Tulsa, I was preparing myself mentally, and perhaps even slipping into a bit of trance, by admiring the effortless flow of the fish. The area in which we would focus on would not be a walk in the park, but nothing compared to what I experienced in Austin. Just as we were about to begin, my eyes locked in on it.

The black biker jacket had been there all along, but I hadn't actually *seen* it until now. No question it was authentic. No doubt it had endured its share of long and dusty highway miles. I appreciated its quality because I had gone through a rather intense leather phase at one point in my life. In those days, I'd have paid a king's ransom to own the distressed garment hanging casually before me. But it wasn't the leather or the shiny buckles dangling from the belt that flipped a switch inside of me. It was the lettering on the back of the coat that struck me as vaguely familiar. Where had I seen that style before? Then it came to me.

"The lettering on your jacket looks like Hell's Angels lettering. Very cool." It was simply a compliment. I wasn't necessarily expecting a response. Certainly not the one I received, anyway.

"Should look real. It *is* Hell's Angels lettering."

Five, maybe six seconds passed while I silently sorted through the barrage of questions that were now swirling around in my mind. Spend ten years on the red carpet of Hollywood's biggest events and you're blessed and cursed with the most inquisitive of minds. I see the potential for an interview in every encounter.

Through my peripheral vision, I examined the man who was of little interest to me less than a minute ago. Now, as he sat close enough for me to feel his hot breath on my arm, he had the potential of being one of the ten most fascinating individuals I'd ever meet. As the buzzing of the tattoo machine sawed on, I seized the opportunity.

"I guess you're a member?" A harmless, non-offensive question. If there were some secret code of silence in place among the brotherhood he could simply choose to ignore me or change the subject. I would take no offense. But, on the other hand, if he wanted to spill his guts I was all ears.

"Not officially," he replied. "When I first opened the shop a few years ago, some of the guys came in to have some work done. I got to know them a little bit."

He then shared a tale of trade. Bartering as we know it dates back thousands of years. I've bartered. You've bartered. Who hasn't, at one time or another, traded a baseball card or an old toy for something more interesting?

According to the artist's story, these particular Hell's Angels members were seeking some rather extensive portrait work. There are very few artists who do that type of tattooing and it comes at a premium price, up to three hundred dollars or more per hour. And it is not a quick process. A detailed picture can often take upwards of eight to ten hours to complete.

Not willing to invest such steep amount, the bikers made a counteroffer: if the artist would agree to provide the requested work, the club would issue him an official Hell's Angel jacket and, even more significant, grant him the freedom to use the traditional (and trademarked) Hell's Angel font, commonly referred to as Bone.

A tiny percentage of the work I've accumulated on my body is the result of some sort of trade. There's no shame in it. You have something I want: a nice tattoo, and I have something you want: exposure in a tattoo trade magazine, for instance. If an honest swap was good enough for the Mesopotamia tribes, it's good enough for me.

But striking a deal with the Hell's Angels was no easy feat. The club boasts three thousand members worldwide and is now run more as a major corporate entity than a biker gang. I knew from my experiences in branding that receiving such a blessing would require more than a handshake. The artist would have been required to pay attorney fees and gather multiple signatures from high up on the food chain before being able to so much as trace the cherished lettering.

Assuming this was just another case of tattoo parlor bragging, I sank deeper into the cracked leather of the old barber chair he used as a tattoo seat and began to get lost in the gentle, hypnotic sting of his machine.

People always seem to want to know if getting a tattoo is painful. There is an air of mystery and rebellion to the art. Therefore, each piece must come with a price. A price many will not want to pay. Anything you're going to have forever requires a little sacrifice, right? So the answer is: *Hell yes they hurt!* That deep, bold ink isn't penetrating your skin with a crayon. The tattoo machine an artist uses on my body has a needle that pops my skin anywhere between fifty to three thousand times per minute. The average sitting is two or three hours from start to finish. Is it painful? Do the math.

I've never put much stock in the type of counseling in which one person walks into the office of another person, pays that person money to unload everything he or she feels uncomfortable or self-conscious about in their lives, and then expects the other person to have the answers. How can that possibly be a sustainable solution to a problem when we're all living in the same world and made up of the same ingredients? Regardless of our backgrounds, no one person is so superior or better adjusted to what life dishes out that they are qualified to "help" another see a better way. That's nonsense to me.

Tattoo therapy is different. No one sits on a higher pedestal than another and pretends to have the answers, There's no judgement or accusations. To me, it's more a form of meditation. I often close my eyes and reach a deeper state of consciousness. Time flies by as the image is being created on my skin.

I mentioned the discussions that often occur in tattoo shops and how they should qualify as therapeutic. There is no question they are much more enlightening and authentic than what you will find in any shrink's office. We all arrive at wherever we are thanks to a series of decisions, circumstances, and consequences. It's interesting to think about where we'd be if we had chosen left instead of right at one of life's crossroads or if we'd stayed with a particular person instead of leaving. Wherever you have been brought you here, and that's the way it was meant to be. I don't believe it's any more complicated than that. I don't go for the higher power philosophy or that everything necessarily happens for a reason. I don't see how a master plan can be possible when so many decisions are left to be made. I subscribe to the thinking that each of us carries around this incredibly powerful tool called the brain. This glorious machine never stops analyzing, processing, and observing. Everything we see, hear, and experience is valuable data that is uploaded to the most sophisticated computer ever designed. The result of all of this information is spit out in the form of instincts, thoughts, and decisions that determine our actions. So when you have two people from different corners of the globe who were brought up by completely different sets of parents in households with opposing viewpoints and their paths somehow intersect in a Tulsa tattoo parlor, you've got the makings of a vibrant interaction.

Because of the angle my arm was positioned in it wasn't possible for me to see how far along my new horseshoe was or, as is many times the case, to judge how much work I'd have to endure until it was complete. The entire process of acquiring a new tattoo is invigorating and there are few things more visually spirited than the colors of a fresh piece, but sit in the same position for two hours for any reason and one tends to grow a little fidgety. In addition to the time, money, and pain, your new tattoo requires patience.

In addition to my growing restlessness, I was beginning to feel the rumblings of hunger. Some of my friends had sent a text inviting me to join them for a late night dinner, and though I would not be able to attend, it was sounding more appealing to me by the minute. I didn't even realize I was hungry until the suggestion of a midnight feast lit up the screen of my iPhone.

I was suddenly awakened from my dream of herb-crusted salmon with a side of garlic mashed potatoes and broccoli au gratin by the haunting creak of shop's thick oak door. My first thought being that it was pretty late for another walk-in appointment.

The two giant men made no attempt to keep the door from slamming. Their long legs covered the distance to the fish tank in less than five easy strides. The thick soles of their boots sounded as if they might plow right through the wood flooring with each step. Standing side by side with their shoulders less than six inches apart, their frames blocked any hope of light from the streetlamp outside from making its way to where I sat. Looking up at them sideways from the barber chair, their massive bulk reminded me of a visit to the Giant Forest in Sequoia National Park.

The scenario I was formulating in my mind would have been complete had the two beasts then pulled out pistols and started shooting the place up. All that was needed for the stereotype to come full circle was for them to violently kick over all of the expensive equipment and dump the fish tank over onto the floor before making their escape to the sounds of approaching police sirens.

But life is rarely as exciting as what we see on the movie screen. In reality, the two men displayed welcoming smiles which made the disturbing images in my head vanish into thin air. Clearly their mothers had raised them right as they both said hello and introduced themselves before slapping the artist on the back taking seats on a worn couch to my left. These men were Nebraska gentlemen through and through, and they were Hell's Angels.

Sure enough, the man coloring in my skin had been telling me the truth. No fabrication. No exaggeration. Sitting with their feet propped up on the coffee table three feet away from me were two honest-to-goodness bikers. Weekend rebels with short, well-maintained haircuts and neatly trimmed beards. They smelled of cologne rather than cigarettes and whiskey. It was a far cry from the outlaw image Hunter S. Thompson wrote of in 1966. Not at all what I expected, if I was expecting anything at all.

Still, these were not the type of guys I wanted as witnesses as a horseshoe was drilled into my arm. I suddenly felt self-conscious when one of them asked what I was getting. Why couldn't they have been in Austin when I was displaying all of that testicular fortitude?

I laughed slightly as I heard myself begin to stumble over my words. Perhaps a dagger through a heart would have made me feel more on par with their masculinity. Somehow the bright orange and yellow color combo I had been so excited about an hour before was making me feel like less of a man. I might as well have been getting Minnie Mouse tattooed on my lower back while enjoying a pedicure. But my self-consciousness did not seem to register with them and they both leaned in to have a look.

After giving an approving nod they moved right along to the next topic of conversation.

These two behemoths had stopped by this tattoo parlor on this night for the same reason I drop in unannounced at Studio 21 in Las Vegas or Inksane Asylum in St. Louis; just to shoot the bull and be among other men. A tattoo shop is a place where boys can be boys. We can cuss, burp, and break wind without consequence. We can give our take on the world's events without interruption. Debates ensue and good-natured harassment is prevalent, but it's all taken in stride.

Despite how they are often perceived, may of us find a tattoo parlor to be a place of solace and repose. A haven where accessibility to one's true self is the norm. And as I discovered in Tulsa, they can also become a place where there are no strangers…only friends yet to meet.

CHAPTER 9

YOU CAN'T GO OUT THERE ALONE

Monday, January 18, 2016, was a sad day for music lovers everywhere. It was Martin Luther King Day. The kids were off school and I was sitting on my couch catching up on shows I had stored on my DVR before hitting the road for the upcoming *TPIR Live* tour. All seemed right with the world until I picked up my phone to check the weather forecast for St. Louis.

Not that the weather in St. Louis affects me one way or the other. It hasn't for a very long time and probably never will again. But my parents had just boarded a plane headed back to the Gateway City after visiting for a few days and I knew the warm temperatures of the west coast would not be following them back to the Midwest. I was right.

While I was kicking back Arizona in flip flops and my favorite t-shirt, their teeth were chattering in temperatures below freezing. But that wasn't the worst news my iPhone was waiting to deliver. According to one of my news apps, an Eagle had passed away.

Glenn Frey was a founding member of what I consider to be one of the most influential and enduring bands in music history. The Beatles have never been my thing and I can take the Rolling Stones or leave them. But if you're riding shotgun in my car and an Eagles tune comes on the radio you'd best just sit tight and take it in because no one touches the dial when *Lyin' Eyes* is playing.

Social media, in my opinion, is the most watered-down source of news. Hoaxes are not uncommon and users are more concerned with appearing relevant and timely to their circle of friends than actually spreading the truth. I was hoping against hope that the headlines that were trending were either unconfirmed or rumors at best. Sadly, they were neither.

The impact the Eagles had on the entertainment industry is monumental, but I cannot say they changed my life. The first contest I ever won on the radio was a pair of tickets to see Don Henley's solo tour in 1985, but picking those tickets up at the radio station was not an indication of the direction my career would eventually take. Like millions of other fans, I felt like I could relate to the words they sang, the harmonies they kept, and the middle-of-the-road melodies. *Desperado*, *Peaceful, Easy Feelin'*, and *Hotel California* are really well-done songs, but I've never felt those songs were written about me. I just liked the way they sounded and it saddens me that the road has come to an end when there seemed to be so much magic left within them.

I never got to see the Eagles in concert. I suppose I came close a time or two, but their tickets were always astronomically expensive and not all that easy to get your hands on. All the more reason why I am proud to say that I had the opportunity to meet Glenn Frey in 2014 at the Mid-America Emmy Awards in Kansas City, MO. That night turned out to be more memorable for me than sitting front row and getting hit in the forehead with a Joe Walsh guitar pick.

In the interest of complete transparency, the local Emmy ceremony was not something I was looking forward to hosting. I had attended the event in the early nineties when my then girlfriend was nominated and found the evening to be poorly structured and far too lengthy. It had not improved much when I was first asked to host in 1999. Although it was an opportunity to return home to St. Louis and spend time with family, it quickly became evident that this party was not going to be what I had grown accustomed to in my few short years in Los Angeles.

I had been covering the red carpet for E! Entertainment Television for three years and had witnessed the glitz and glamor of the Academy Awards, the Grammy Awards, and the Emmys. I had watched the private rehearsals of the American Music Awards as Dick Clark himself covered every inch of the stage making performance suggestions to mega-acts like the Backstreet Boys and Foo Fighters. The power of preparation meeting with the magic of performance was demonstrated to me time and time again. Perfection at that level is not random. David Letterman used to refer to his off-the-cuff moments as "rehearsed spontaneity." As I've said many, many times before; hosting is more than Crest White Strips and spray tans. The hours of practice that go into making sure a crew was ready became a way of life. So when the confidence that stems from such hard work is absent, it is immediately noticeable to me. Something was missing in Missouri.

The moment I stepped foot into the Grand Ballroom of St. Louis' majestic Union Station I felt an emptiness that would encompass the evening ahead of me. Other than the eight foot Emmy statues bookending the stage, there was no visible grandeur. Nothing to spotlight or celebrate the achievements of the men and women who work their asses off writing, editing, and delivering the local news night after night. In fact, walking through those doors made me feel like I was the first to arrive at a wedding reception. No one was there to greet me. The lights were down. The sound had not been set up. We were less than six hours from showtime and the only people ready to go to work were myself and the serving staff who were busy setting the tables.

Originally opened in 1894, Union Station is still one of St. Louis' proudest architectural achievements. The clock tower rises prominently above the skyline on Market Street and the Grand Hall, which was completely renovated in 2014, treats visitors to sweeping archways and beautiful art glass windows that allow us to take a peek back in time.

Sadly, not many people visit Union Station anymore. An attempt in the late eighties to convert the once thriving train station into a touristy shopping experience failed miserably. In fact, to walk through its vast hallways today, one would never know it once was a major transportation hub for all of the Midwest. A retail presence is barely visible. Storefronts remain empty after businesses flee for greener pastures and Union Station has become a sorrowful, cavernous place to visit.

After making numerous inquiries with the mall staff, I was finally approached by a producer of the show. With time being such a factor, I was surprised when, rather than take the stage for soundcheck, we hastily went through the script while sitting on a wood bench in the lobby.

Either through naivety or blatant deception, my young producer chose that moment to inform me that there would be no teleprompter. This translated to mean that everything I was to deliver to the audience that night would either need to be memorized within the next few hours or read right off the paper I held in my hands. Fortunately, I had hired the services of my friend, comedy writer Peter Charkalis. This is a common practice among hosts at award shows. Writers are brought in to spice the evening up with topical, yet subtle humor. Knowing I had some substance to fall back on made me a bit more comfortable with the less than desirable situation that had just been dumped in my lap.

I graciously shook her hand and thanked her before retreating to my hotel room. I wanted to prepare as much as I could in the little time I had. Knowing full well that the host is the face of the show, my head needed to be right for the night ahead. When a ceremony like the Emmy Awards is criticized for lacking pizazz, the host takes the arrows. I accept that responsibility. It comes with the territory. But my plan for that evening in St. Louis centered around keeping things moving. One has to expect acceptance speeches to drag on. We are powerless in that respect. The winners deserve their moment in the spotlight, just like I deserved mine in 2012, but aside from the awards I wanted the audience to associate my presence on stage with energy and light-heartedness.

And so it was. Throughout the night I was sharp. I was polite. And I was pleasant. After just under three hours of sitting uncomfortably in lightly-padded banquet chairs, the black tie and evening gown-clad audience made their way to the bar while I made my way back to my room to get some sleep. As is my routine, I simply wadded up my tuxedo and tossed it into my suitcase. I'd let the dry cleaner back home worry about the wrinkles. My priority was getting into bed as soon as possible before my early flight back to Los Angeles. My final thought of the night being:

"That went better than expected, but I'll never do it again."

"Sure, Maggie. I'd be honored to host the show this year."

Look, we all have the right to change our minds. It's what sets humans apart from grasshoppers. Our points of view change with the seasons. You meet someone at a dinner party and she's everything you've ever wanted. Three days later you take her to a baseball game and you're praying to a god you don't believe in for the nachos in your lap to give you food poisoning so you can cut the date short. You see a pair of shoes that you *must* own and come to realize a year later that you never once put them on your feet. We all deserve cooling off periods and a little leeway when it comes to altering our opinions. As a result of my recent, slightly matured outlook on things, I accepted an invitation to return as host of the Mid-America Emmys in 2014.

The show was now being produced by two people whom I adore. The first is the lovely Maggie Eubanks. Maggie is a people person and a stickler for detail. She runs a tight ship with a friendly hand and it's always a pleasure to be in her company.

Serving as the stage producer would be my longtime friend, Tom Rogers. Tom and I have a fruitful history together and I consider him to be one of those people I would do just about anything for. Because I knew and respected both Tom and Maggie, I felt confident the 2014 show would be an entirely different experience than 1999.

My first exposure to a television camera came in 1992. I was already on top of the St. Louis airwaves. Using the moniker Rick Idol, I was leading the pack. Our radio station, WKBQ, was a ratings monster and the advertisers we had on board were spending boatloads of money on commercial time, sponsorships, and appearances. We were out on the streets shaking hands and kissing babies from dusk till dawn, and our extraordinary Arbitron numbers were a reflection of the effort the entire staff put into the station's success. No team of radio professionals has ever worked harder or more in tune with one another than we did from 1992-1994. When I returned to the St. Louis airwaves for a brief stint in 2015, I noticed right away how things had changed. The magic wasn't there. The enthusiasm wasn't there. The belief in our product wasn't there. But in 1992, the pride in the work we were doing was unmistakable. In fact, it was infectious.

The local FOX affiliate took notice of the impact WKBQ (Q104) was having on the younger demographics. Men and women between the ages of eighteen to twenty-five felt that all important connection with the music we were playing and the image we were portraying. All of the personalities were seen as good timing guys and gals who were still able to make it work the next day. We were where you wanted to be and who you wanted to be with. As a result of the station's enormous popularity, I received a phone call one Tuesday morning that would ultimately change the course of my career.

Tom Rogers was, and is at the time of this writing, one of the most revered producers in the St. Louis market. He has always been a forward thinker and a creative genius. When the local FOX affiliate needed to cut a series of public service announcements (PSA's) encouraging teenagers to select a designated driver on graduation night, Tom's vision led him to pick up the phone and call the young hotshot DJ that all the kids were listening to every evening. We enjoyed working together so much on that project, and it proved to be so effective in its mission, that he reached out to me again a few months later to tape some vignettes promoting the channel's afternoon programming slot. This opportunity brought massive amounts of exposure my way as the lineup included such hit shows as *The Simpsons* and *Friends*. The synergy Tom and I created made his job at the TV station easier and made my radio show even more popular by introducing me to an even broader audience. The world is a wonderful rock to be on when everyone wins.

When I learned Tom would be stage managing the 2014 show, I didn't hesitate to return. The stage manager is who sees to it that the host is where he or she needs to be when he or she needs to be there. We rely heavily upon our stage managers to handle the details and to make us shine like stars.

There is no shortage of things that can go wrong during a live event. We all witnessed the 2015 Miss Universe debacle when Steve Harvey mishandled the pinnacle of the evening, the announcement of the winner. It is my firm belief that mishap stemmed from the host not feeling comfortable and confident. Steve Harvey is an incredibly talented man, but being on a stage of that size when you haven't rehearsed and prepared yourself for any and all outcomes is like walking the streets of New York City wearing a blindfold. You may make it to where you want to go, but it isn't going to be easy.

With Tom as my producer, I knew I would have a safety net in the event something slipped off course. He would see to it that all of my scripts were in the teleprompter, that all presenters were standing by when I introduced them, and that my zipper wasn't down before I walked on stage. And because I always memorize my scripts in bullet point fashion I would not be left out in the cold. I learned that lesson after a technical mishap in San Juan back in '01.

Co-hosting the 2001 Miss Universe pageant was going to be the biggest and most widely-viewed broadcast of my career. Not only would the telecast be seen by nearly a billion people worldwide, but I would be sharing the stage with supermodels Elle Macpherson and Naomi Campbell. Needless to say, my professional stock would rise if I was seen as someone who could hold his own alongside such big names. The publicity surrounding the original gender of one of the contestants only added to the hype and made this particular pageant one of the most anticipated shows in television history.

When my then agent Greg Horangic contacted me with the opportunity to be a part of this massive production, I must admit I was reluctant to accept. Of course I wanted to be there, but Silver was nearly eight months pregnant with Mason and I could not justify jetting off to beautiful Puerto Rico to work with the world's most dazzling women while my wife endured the final trimester of her first pregnancy back in California.

My gut was telling me it wasn't the right thing to do, and my gut never has never lied to me.

I will not pretend to believe my agent had my best interests at heart when he encouraged me to accept the hosting role. He, of course, would collect a nice commission and any high profile show a client gets is good for the company. But Greg knew Silver and certainly understood my apprehension. Fortunately, I was able to make peace with the situation and, thanks to one very powerful and influential man, we were able to do the deal.

Donald Trump owned a significant portion of the Miss Universe Organization at the time. When word of my concerns got back to the executives at the Trump Organization, special accommodations were made to make the agreement work.

First, Silver would now be joining me on the trip to San Juan. With her doctor's blessing, we were able to fly in a day or two later than originally planned and depart immediately following the broadcast, thus minimizing our time away from home. Second, the Trump Organization saw to it that we had a town car and a local driver available to us around the clock should we need to get to a hospital.

We were also given the private numbers of a local obstetrician should Mason decide he'd like to be born in a tropical paradise rather than Cedars Sinai. Every single concern we had was addressed, leaving us no choice but to accept the coveted co-hosting position. I'd never felt so cared for and appreciated. It was the perfect example of how taking care of your people builds loyalty and inspires superior performance. I am grateful to Mr. Trump for his kindness and understanding of our delicate and personal situation.

With every detail covered it was time to board the plane and focus on doing the best job possible. Upon arriving at Luis Muñoz Marín International Airport in San Juan, I was presented with my call sheets and show packet. I would be rehearsing for hours while she basked in the sun by the pool in a maternity swimsuit we picked up in Beverly Hills especially for the trip.

The Host With The Most

During one of my breaks, I stepped out of the arena where musical guest Ricky Martin was rehearsing and went to join my wife for a little fresh air. I had to smile as I approached and witnessed no fewer than five Miss Universe delegates and their sponsors gushing over my pregnant bride telling her how beautiful she looked. The Donald even stopped by to say hello and offer his good wishes. Obviously Silver was in good hands and any second thoughts I may have been harboring were washed away.

The abundance of rehearsal time we put in paid off in spades. During one of our live spots in which I was interviewing contestants backstage following the swimsuit competition, my teleprompter just went black. There was nothing showing on the screen. Not a single word was visible. But the little red light glowing brightly let me know that there were still millions of people watching me. The show must go on. Thanks to the run thru's the top-notch crew and I had been subjected to, I knew what I needed to say and where the segment was meant to go. My job was to get the reactions of the contestants then lead us to Ricky's performance. His single "Livin' la Vida Loca" was the biggest hit on the radio and he was standing by, waiting for my cue. And you can believe got us there.

With Donald Trump standing behind the camera watching me every step of the way, viewers at home had no idea we had endured a technical snafu. The power of preparation had once again prevailed. When Ricky hit his first note, everyone backstage burst into applause and congratulated one another on a job well done.

As my stage manager was leading me back to the stage to rejoin Elle and Naomi, Mr. Trump patted me on the shoulder and said, "Wonderful job." That meant a lot to me. I knew how much money Mr. Trump had invested in this telecast and how much pride he took in it. In fact, I was so moved by his kindness and impressed by the work ethic he inspired in others that it played a major part in an important decision I made in 2015.

This Miss USA pageant had fallen under severe scrutiny over statements Donald Trump made in the early stages of his bid for the Republican presidential nomination. With the pageant just days away, Macy's, NBC, and other corporate backers began pulling out after The Donald made some comments about Mexican immigrants that many found offensive and in poor taste. It is not my place to say whether they were or they weren't. As I've stated in interview after interview, I am not defined by the words or actions of another. As a registered Libertarian I believe in speaking and acting for myself. We live in a free country and the First Amendment allows anyone to speak his or her mind. If others become offended, then let a discussion take place. But I was not interested in allowing politics and the government into my personal life any more than they already were.

What did interest me was a phone call I received in early June of that year. I was spending the afternoon on Cape Cod when a representative from The Miss Universe Organization called to see if I would be interested in stepping into the host role for the upcoming Miss USA pageant in Baton Rouge, LA. The previous hosts had bowed out in fear of being associated with Trump and I was next on their list.

I, of course, seized the opportunity with little hesitation. Fully aware that there would be at least a mild amount of backlash, I told myself that a host should be a host, and because of Mr. Trump this would be one of the most talked about pageants since Miss Universe in '01. A pass would mean I would miss out on a ripe opportunity to show my live hosting skills to a larger audience than I had in years and expose the new generation of casting agents and producers to what The Host with the Most® can do on a stage of such epic proportions.

I accepted the offer the caller proposed without even contacting my manager. The money was secondary. First and foremost I would be front and center at the show the entire nation was buzzing about. I immediately shared the news with my family and that evening we celebrated by ordering take out from our favorite pizza joint.

Not everyone was as excited about my decision as I was. A handful of people threw halfhearted jabs and called me names like "traitor" and "sellout" on social media, but those people are easily ignored. Overall, the support was extremely positive and never once did I second guess my instincts. What was most flattering was the fact that TMZ covered the announcement on their nightly show and called me "the man brought in to pick up the pieces." I took that as a huge compliment.

The professional courtesy that Donald Trump and his staff showed me nearly fifteen years before had not been forgotten. Regardless of what people were saying about him at the time of Miss USA, I knew what I had seen and experienced of him firsthand and that is what my decision to step in among the turmoil was based upon. I was taught to make my own choices and to stand on my own two feet. I'm proud of the decision I made and even more proud of the show that we put on. The pageant was dropped picked up by REELZ Channel where it went on to garner some of the highest ratings in the network's history.

There's no denying the natural ability involved in hosting. There's natural ability involved in any occupation. A car salesperson must have a God-given knack for overcoming a potential customer's objections. A doctor must possess a calming bedside manner. And a host needs to be able to fly by the seat of his or her pants if necessary. But it is the responsibility of the individual to take what Mother Nature has given you and cultivate it into performance excellence. Michael Jordan is a genetic wonder, but hours upon hours spent in gymnasiums and the guidance of countless coaches molded him into the superstar we know him to be. The same can be said for actors like Al Pacino or Meryl Streep. Painters like Michelangelo. Musicians like Dave Grohl or Luciano Pavarotti. Success requires hustle. And I believe a lack of hustle, not a lack of ability, is to blame for the Miss Universe 2015 mishap. The team was in place, but the ball was dropped just as Steve Harvey was rushing into the end zone. Success is not a guarantee.

Contrary to my experience in 1999, rehearsal time was not in short supply when it came to the 2014 Mid-America Emmy Awards. As stated before, Tom Rogers and I were more than comfortable with each other's work patterns, and we also had the luxury of sharing an incredible chemistry. TR informed me that I would have as much or as little leeway as I needed to keep the flow of the evening's performance in check. That was all I needed to hear. If a winner happened to go over the allotted time for her acceptance speech, I would keep my bit concise. Alternatively, if people began flying through their time on stage, which is normal when one is nervous or excited, I had the affordability of going out into the audience and filling time with banter and interaction.

With Tom at my side, I took the stage of the great Kansas City Music Hall on the afternoon of the ceremony solely for the purpose of reading through teleprompter copy. Several sponsors had coughed up quite a bit of money to make the event happen and we wanted to ensure their moment in the spotlight was accurate and smooth. The read thru took just under and hour and Tom and I were about to leave to have lunch in KC's Power & Light District when the evening's guest of honor arrived to practice his portion of the show.

Each year, this division of the National Academy of Television Arts and Sciences presents the prestigious Governor's Award to a man or woman from the region who has achieved a level of professional excellence in the television and/or radio industry. This particular year, at the 38th annual ceremony, that honor would be bestowed upon Springfield, MO, native Les Garland.

Les is a man who has done it all in the world of broadcast entertainment. Known primarily as the innovative co-founder of MTV, he is a radio pioneer who broke many influential artists and went on to become the head of AfterPlay Entertainment. Most impressive to me, however, is the fact that it is Les' voice that is heard as the DJ in Jefferson Starship's number one song "We Built This City."

Each Governor's Award recipient is encouraged to invite his or her own presenter. Often it is the spouse who stood by the winner's side for decades or the children who inspired his or her drive. Perhaps it is a mentor or a partner without whom such achievements would not have been possible. But Les Garland took it to an entirely new and unexpected level. Les showed up at our quiet little rehearsal with none other than the legendary Glenn Frey.

The Eagles, again, is arguably one of the most influential rock & roll bands in music history. With moving lyrics and incomparable harmonies, Glenn and bandmates Don Henley, Joe Walsh, Timothy B. Schmit, and

Randy Meisner defined the American landscape in the 1970's and represented the California lifestyle to people worldwide. To see him casually walk through the door in a t-shirt, jeans, and boots and silently wait for instruction from Tom was almost too much for me to handle.

I've interviewed them all. From Bill Clinton to Oprah, and from Schwarzenegger to Stan Musial, there aren't too many names or faces that are capable of leaving me starstruck. I had never even considered how I would react to being in the presence of an Eagle, especially in such a casual setting, but I can honestly say I was caught off guard. In fact, Tom and I both were. Les Garland had not informed anyone who he would be bringing, but his choice in presenters made perfect sense.

The Eagles considered Les not only a dear friend, but a driving force in the band's early success. Les was the first to hear that special something in their sound and to release it to the masses via the airwaves of the radio stations he programmed. Les believed in the band as much as the actual members did and the result was a lifelong friendship.

Seeing Glenn and Les interact with one another was like watching two high school buddies. There was no doubt of the strength of their bond. It was fun to observe. Rarely does one see such a megastar in his or her natural habitat. It was refreshing, in a sense. This man was a musical genius. A Grammy winner six times over. A multi-millionaire. A poet extraordinaire. One of the most famous faces and voices in the world. And he was sitting two feet from me in an empty Kansas City banquet room.

A funny thing happens when you are in the presence of a celebrity. Within a span of just a few seconds, you see in your mind's eye a montage of every instance where that person has entered your space. I flashed back to 1988 when my best friend Matt Stricklin and I would blast the cassette single of *Heartache Tonight* on our way to school each morning. I remembered sitting in a London pub with a woman named Jody. We discussed the meaning of the lyrics to *Hotel California* until the sun came up. And most vividly, I could close my eyes and see Silver rocking both of our children to sleep as she hummed the melody to *Peaceful, Easy Feeling* to them. In an instant, seeing Glenn in person brought all of these beautiful images back.

Glenn Frey was approachable and accommodating. Anything that needed to be done to make the most of his friend's moment he was willing to do. When he was comfortable with his role for the evening and had received all of his stage directions, he and Les said their goodbyes and left the room. Tom and I stood silently for a moment before turning to one another and busting out in giddy laughter like a couple of starstruck schoolgirls. Did that just happen?

It was only a few hours later, after a long lunch and a short nap, that I found myself back in the same ballroom where I had encountered royalty earlier that afternoon. Now, however, I was decked out in a tuxedo and saying hello to former colleagues from the St. Louis television market. Everyone looked spectacular as an air of nervous energy lingered throughout. Being presented with an Emmy Award means something in show business. It doesn't matter if it is a local Emmy, a Daytime Emmy, or a Primetime Emmy when you take home the gold people know your name. For that one moment in time you are the very best at what you do. For me it represented a culmination of everything I had done in my life leading up to that moment. Sacrificing personal time in lieu of going the extra mile, working for peanuts, shadowing those who were where I wanted to be. Suddenly it seemed as if it had all been worthwhile. I enjoyed sharing the anxiety and anticipation of the nominees that I had the pleasure of meeting before needing to get backstage for last minute notes. The pressure was all on them. All I needed to do was flash my smile and recite my lines. Tom Rogers would handle the rest.

Les Garland was scheduled to receive his award approximately one hour into the ceremony. When he and Glenn arrived through a back hallway, they were ushered to our small waiting area where we would hold until Tom came to get us. The space was approximately eight feet by ten feet and curtained off with black draping. Seating consisted not of the plush couches I'm certain Glenn must be used to having in a green room, but of five folding metal chairs. It was apparent no one in the audience had the slightest inkling that Glenn was in the building, otherwise there would be crowds gathering just on the other side of the curtain hoping for a glance. The staff and crew had somehow managed to keep it under wraps, and he certainly would not be spotted buried there in the darkest corner of the room.

At one point in the evening, there were only four of us occupying the tiny area: myself, Glenn, Les, and a young female college student hired by a local modeling agency to act as the trophy girl for the evening. Her role consisted of looking beautiful and handing the Emmy statue to the winner while making sure they exited off to the proper side of the stage.

I was having a nice conversation with Les when, out of the corner of my eye, I noticed the young lady turn to Glenn. I could tell she was uncomfortable with the silence and was just attempting to make polite conversation. For no other reason other than my own curiosity, I leaned in a bit to decipher what this bubbly twenty-something had to say to an Eagle. What I heard instantly became embedded deep within the alcoves of my mind where it would be saved as fact for my next book.

"So, are you are a singer or something?" Les looked at me and smiled. His smirk let me know that he knew Glenn well enough to anticipate nothing short of a stellar comeback. Glenn took a long, slow sip of the complimentary wine we had been provided with backstage. He paused and placed his wine glass on the floor before responding.

"Yes, I'm in a band called the Eagles," Glenn said politely. "Have you heard of us?"

The young lady's face took on a look of great concentration as if she were searching every mental playlist on her internal hard drive. "I don't think so," she responded. "But I'm sure my parents have."

I cringed as Les chuckled. What came next was brilliance that could only flow from the mouth of a man who has sold out stadiums and had more gold hanging on the walls of his home than Fort Knox.

"Well, we're one of the most famous bands in history and we sell out every show we play, but you never hear about that because we've been doing it year after year since the early seventies. Tell your dad you met an Eagle and that Glenn said hello."

The girl nodded and picked up her phone. Being a member of the texting generation, I'm sure it took her all of about eighteen seconds to relay Glenn's greeting to Mom and Dad back home. I would have paid a small fortune to have been a fly on the wall in that Missouri living room when the message came through. They're probably *still* talking about it at Sunday School.

The backstage libations continued to flow as the night rolled on. Nominees were read and winners were announced. The Governor's Award presentation could not come soon enough as I could tell from the stage that the audience was growing restless. Once you've had your picture taken and said all the hellos that are required in an environment consisting of such schmooze, you just want to go home and put on your pajamas. The evening was taking a toll on their patience, but I knew they were about to be blown away by the evening's surprise guest.

I feel it is important to mention that rarely, if ever, do I drink during an event. Consuming alcohol does not play into the image of professionalism I try to maintain, and I strive to stay as sharp and in control as I possibly can. But this night in KC easily qualifies as an exception. It's not often that one can drink cheap wine with Glenn Frey, and therefore I indulged in several hearty sips along with him between each foray onto the stage. I was feeling no pain when it came time for his introduction.

A Broadway-style quartet from Branson, MO, had been booked to provide the evening's live musical entertainment. I can't say they were stellar performers. Their medley of 80's television anthems didn't really bring the house down, but Tom had informed me during our rehearsal that the theme song to *Friends* would be my cue that there was one minute left in their less-than-memorable display.

They sashayed their way through the familiar themes of everything from *The Love Boat* to *Facts of Life*. The audience found a bit of comedic value in the fact that not a single one of the singers appeared to be over the age of twenty-two. Realizing they were not old enough to have suffered through Michael J. Fox's heartbreaking split from Courtney Cox on *Family Ties* tainted the entire presentation with the stench of inauthenticity.

Nonetheless, I recognized the opening chords of The Rembrandts' "I'll Be There For You" and began making my way to the side of the stage. The effects of the wine led me to pay special attention to every move I made, so I let Glenn know that I'd be introducing him as a special guest and would let the impact of his surprise appearance take the audience by storm as it had me. He nodded as if to say he was up for anything.

Keep It Simple, Stupid (KISS) is a good rule of thumb. It's not always the flashiest way to deliver a presentation or make an introduction, but it is historically failsafe. It was also the method I chose to introduce Glenn Frey.

"Ladies and Gentlemen, we have reached a very special part of the evening…the presentation of this year's Governor's Award. And as I am sure you'll agree, such a special honor deserves nothing less than a very special presenter. If you would, a nice round of applause for tonight's very special guest."

As I walked offstage, Glenn Frey, a master of timing and rhythm, stood in the wings allowing the natural anticipation of the audience to reach a crescendo. Unaware of who they were about to meet, the applause from the crowd was polite yet unenthusiastic. Ever the performer, Glenn saw it for what it was and allowed the wonder of the moment to simmer.

I passed on his left to allow him plenty of room to make his way up the stairs. Just as I reached the floor, Glenn said, "Todd, would you mind handing me my wine glass?"

I picked it up and handed it over assuming he was looking to take one last swig. But without missing a beat, he lifted the glass to me and said, "Thanks. Can't go out there alone, ya know?"

And then Glenn Frey delivered the most heartfelt speech about his friend anyone could imagine.

It was an honor for all who were in attendance to watch and listen to Glenn Frey. He moved us with his words and electrified us with his charisma. Every man and woman in that audience took something valuable home with them that night. For some, it was a Mid-America Emmy Award. For others, it was a great story about being able to shake the hand of their favorite singer. Me? Well, I left the Kansas City Music Hall with something more special than both of those things combined. I left with Glenn Frey's wine glass.

Cheers to you, Glenn.

CHAPTER 10

CONFESSIONS OF A PIZZA DELIVERY BOY

I suppose the time has come for me to face the truth. Facts are facts and I need to step up and accept the harsh reality that I just was not meant for the food service industry. Not by a long shot. My brief foray into the restaurant business provided all the evidence needed to conclude that we are all meant to assume different roles and I know what side of the counter I belong on.

I'm a man who loves going out to dinner. I plan in advance, read reviews, and make reservations. The experience of fine dining is my indulgence of choice. Enjoying different cuisines as I travel internationally makes me feel as if I'm getting a genuine taste for the culture. My horizons expand as rapidly as my waistline and I justify such sittings as reward for my hard work .

I will pay top dollar for top service and I tip generously when it is deserving, but I will not hesitate to express my displeasure when things do not live up to my expectations. A restaurant only receives rave reviews when they meet the standards of guests and critics, which is why a quality establishment seeks only to hire the very best. The very best hostesses, the very best servers, the very best chefs. But here and now I have publicly come to terms with the fact that no restaurant, anywhere in the world, would every consider me to be the very best. Not ever.

For those who have read my book, *Life In The Bonus Round*, you may recall my telling of the infamous Burger King kitchen fire. In what was my first (and last) shift at the fast food chain, inexperience and lack of interest nearly led me to burn the place to the ground. I only wish that was an exaggeration. I accept full blame as I failed to drain the scolding hot oil from the fryers before turning them off to clean them at the end of the night. The result was an eye-opening three to four-foot flame protruding from the stainless steel contraption and shrieks of horror from my co-workers. I thought parading around in the rust-colored uniform was cause enough for ridicule, but the look of shock and helplessness on my face must have been the cherry on top.

My first inclination upon seeing the small inferno was feverishly begin turning this knob and that in hopes of disconnecting the power or closing the gas line. I frantically pushed every button and swiped everything worth swiping. Beepers were beeping and lights were flashing yet nothing would cause the flame to retreat. I began to sweat, both from the heat and from the shame. The fire maintained its taunting dance. Someone needed to step in and do something or this situation was going to get dangerously out of hand.

During our training at Whopper College, my fellow recruits and I were reminded time and again that a supervisor is on hand at all times. Should we ever have a question or should an issue arise with a customer, we were always to contact the supervisor right away. Well, I had a question: *How do I keep this place from becoming a pile of burnt onion rings?* I also had an issue: Fire!

He stood all of five feet and five inches tall. I know that for certain because my mother is the same height and his head met the same spot on my chest as her's did. In spite of being vertically challenged, he was clearly the man in charge because unlike the rest of us who were dressed in smocks, my manger sported a button down shirt and a name tag of a different color. The executive look. I don't know what type of executive training is required to reach such a coveted position in the company, but I hoped included putting out fryer fires.

Jumping into action with a clear sense of urgency, he bumped me out of the way as he knelt before the fryer. His bravery was impressive as he reached into the bowels of the smoldering machine. Thankfully there was an emergency disconnect that put an end to the chaos almost immediately. Logic would suggest we all be made aware of such a failsafe, but the man in charge was the sole possessor of such knowledge. Disaster averted.

The restaurant became deathly quiet as the pandemonium subsided. All eyes made their way to me. I alone was the culprit. Desperately searching for a way to redeem my self worth, I decided to initiate cleanup by lifting the fry baskets up from the fryer and over to a sanitized cleaning area behind me. When in doubt, look busy.

Unfortunately, my attempt to do good made things irretrievably worse. Drops of scalding hot grease directly dripped onto my supervisor's head as I lifted them into the air. Fast forward twenty years to when I lived on top of Mulholland Drive in Los Angeles and would often hear the screeches of nearby coyotes during their midnight feasts. My little boss' yelps of pain were of equal pitch and volume.

"Just get the hell out of here, would ya Tom?" he screamed.

I don't know who Tom was, but neither he nor I ever returned to the scene of the crime except to collect my paycheck; a mere eleven dollars in change. After being so quickly and decisively relieved of my duties and realizing that life didn't look so rosy through the glass of a drive-thru window, I set out in search other means of employment.

If the definition of insanity is doing the same thing over and over and hoping for a different result then I must be crazy. For reasons unbeknownst to me, I felt the need to dust myself off and climb back into the food industry saddle. Some of my basketball teammates were delivering pizzas for a popular family-owned chain called Imo's and there appeared to be an opening at our neighborhood location.

Imo's is a St. Louis institution and my buddies raved about about the fast cash they were pulling in and the pretty private school girls that worked the front counter. I was told that tips were often supplemented by clipping coupons out of the Sunday newspaper and turning them in as if the customer had supplied them. The discounted amount was then added to our delivery pull. Other perks included a free tank of gas at the beginning of each shift and all the pizza we could eat. I mean, what better job could there possibly be for a high school sophomore with a love of money, an endless appetite, and a red Ford Escort that got twenty miles to the gallon?

Keep in mind that being a pizza delivery boy was much more involved in 1986 than it is today. We didn't have the luxury of asking Siri for the best route to a hungry customer's home. We were old school. A *Thomas Guide* a driver's lifesaver back then.

Thick as a phone book, each page of a *Thomas Guide* was an individual map representing a tiny sector of the given city or state. If, while out on delivery, you found yourself driving off the edge of the map you simply needed to turn the page and your journey could continue without interruption.

The book took some getting used to, but time is money and it was worth investing a few minutes here and there to learn how to best utilize it. The faster a driver was able to locate an address the sooner we could drop off the pie and get on to the next house. At the time, Domino's Pizza was guaranteeing all orders would be delivered in thirty minutes or less. They've since realized the dangers associated with hundreds of young male drivers rushing to their destinations under the stress of that promise and have wisely done away with it, but when I was in the game Domino's was the name to beat, and my *Thomas Guide* served as the ideal co-pilot.

Time wasn't all we needed to invest. A *Thomas Guide* can be rather pricey for a kid who works for tips, but staying current when it came to the new subdivisions that were popping up and knowing the winding curves of the rural roads comes at a premium. We never balked at the cost because our only other option left much to be desired.

I can still picture it. A giant, laminated poster of our delivery area hanging there in all of it's greasy glory right next to the back exit through which only the delivery team passed. It was bigger than the Magic Johnson and Heather Thomas posters that hung in my bedroom at the time, and its detail would make NASA jealous. If a customer called from outside the clearly marked region they were politely directed to another location by our meticulous and courteous counter girl, Janet; the oldest of a set of beautiful blonde twins who served not only as one of my first real crushes, but as the first impression of the restaurant.

Janet had worked the phones at Imo's for so long that she didn't even need to look at the map. The boundaries were ingrained on her mind and she could recognize many of our more frequent customers just by the sound of their voices on the phone. She knew addresses by heart and could fill in on the pizza-making line if the store got busy.

Male customers would linger as Janet and her sister Judy hand wrote each order and rang it up with a smile. In fact, I believe Janet and Judy were the pioneers of counter help receiving tips. Today, every coffee shop in the known universe sports a tip jar, but back then it was wasn't commonplace. It was customary to tip servers and delivery drivers, but never the girl at the counter. The twins changed all of that.

Every night husbands and fathers volunteered to run down to Imo's and grab a pizza for the family while wives and children stayed at home. These men never called in advance to save time. They were happy to wait in the lobby while it baked regardless of how backed up our kitchen may have been. They were content to bask in the radiant, youthful glow of the twins.

If you lived out of our service area, however, the girls would make no exceptions to store policy. It was this type of discipline that has kept the delicious thin-crust empire at the top of the pizza chain mountain for decades.

It was a seemingly routine evening. Not too busy and not too slow. No unusual orders. No food fights in the back kitchen. Nothing appeared to be out of the ordinary until Jack, our store manager, asked me if I would mind running a double to keep the kitchen from getting backed up.

The term "double" referred to the occasional need to deliver to more than one location on a single outing. Though not common practice because it risked jeopardizing the freshness of the pie, it can be a necessary evil during the dinner rush that usually resulted in twice the tips for the chosen driver. I wasn't about to miss an opportunity to put a little extra jingle in my pocket, and Janet didn't seem to paying much attention to me anyway, so I slid the two cardboard boxes into the red thermal carrier that would keep them piping hot for the short duration of my ride.

A man needs to have a plan regardless of the type of business he is in. Whether he's managing a hedge fund or bringing someone's dinner to them while they watch a ballgame, it's important to have some idea of what your next move is going to be. As I pulled out of the parking lot of the strip mall that housed our store, I decided I'd run the delivery that was furthest away first and hit the second house on the way back. There was no rhyme or reason to my decision. I wouldn't save any gas or make up any real time with the route I'd chosen. It just seemed to be the right thing to do at the time. But hindsight... well, you know how the saying goes.

The address of my first stop was not one that I recognized. Many street numbers become familiar to drivers over time because pizza customers are a loyal bunch and, let's face it, folks just don't like to cook at home. You begin to associate phone numbers with orders and can even predict what kind of tip you'll leave with based on past experiences. Again, repetition builds reputation. Though this particular street was one I'd delivered to many times before, the white two-story colonial at the end of the cul de sac was a new one for me. Perhaps someone had just relocated to the area or maybe they saw the coupon in the paper and decided to give us a shot. Anyway you looked at it was a chance to lock in a new customer.

I parked my car on the street in front of the house, grabbed the top pizza from the carrier, and made my way up a steep driveway to the front porch. The main door was open behind a screen giving me a clear view into the living room where light from the television danced off of the walls.

A man in his early twenties apparently watched me arrive and invited me inside.

Waiting in the foyer while a customer goes off into another room to retrieve their money is not unusual, especially in inclement weather. Only a heartless soul would leave a teenager standing outside in the snow or rain.

I was admiring the framed family photographs in the hallway when three more men, who had clearly been drinking and were elated that dinner was now being served, offered me a beer and engaged me in meaningless conversation to help pass the time. I thought it a bit odd that when the man who answered the door finally returned, he asked to inspect the pizza before handing over the money. He claimed the last time he placed an order he received what we called a "slider"-a sloppy mess where all of the toppings on the pizza have slid to one side of the box. This is common with drivers who don't pay attention to the position of their carriers when en route and is usually rectified by sending another pizza right out to the customer.

Confident in my skills, I handed the man the box and expected to be given the money in an even exchange. Instead, he opened the lid and instantly his eyes took on a psychotic glare. They seemed to look right into my very soul as he appeared to transform into an entirely different person than the man who invited me in out of the rain. Through clenched teeth, he hissed that his order was wrong.

Even in my teens, I like to think I was bright enough to avoid succumbing to knee-jerk reactions. Practicing patience avoids having to deal with regret. What I wanted to tell him was to sell this scam somewhere else because I wasn't buying, but instead I attempted to respond rationally in hopes of not fanning the flames of an escalating situation.

I looked at the ticket, then up at him, then back down at the ticket. Then, as if presenting evidence to a jury, I compared what Janet had written to the pizza he now held and was refusing to hand back. The two were a perfect match. I was holding the smoking gun. If there was a miscommunication with the order, I was most definitely looking right at the culprit. Janet, after all, did not make careless errors and her bubbly handwriting was meticulous. You don't get to be Employee of the Month six months running by writing pepperoni when it was meant to be Italian sausage.

I felt as if I was doing a pretty convincing job of pleading my case when one of the other men returned to the living room area, took a piece of pizza out of the box, and stuffed it into his mouth. At that point it was abundantly clear that they had no intention of paying me and the battle lines had been drawn. This was a challenging situation that was about to become even worse. My options, what few there were to begin with, became more limited by the second. I was outnumbered, inexperienced, and scared. But even at that young age, I had one thing going for me: the gift of gab.

If I could keep them engaged long enough maybe I could reposition myself closer to the door and make a run for it. Why had I ventured so far into the house? I would have to explain to Jack why I was coming back with no money but at least I wouldn't be beaten to a pulp over a ten dollar pie.

Quickly I decided that if I couldn't dazzle them with brilliance, then I would baffle them with bullshit. The only course of action I could see was to take the attention off of me and give the man I took to be the leader of this gang of fools the respect his parents never had.

"Maybe I could use your phone," I suggested. "We can figure this all out." Doing so, I assured him, would get the correct order on its way to the house much quicker than if I drove back and waited for it. After a moment of consideration, he obliged. Thinking he had the chance to snow us for *two* free pizzas instead of one, he led me into the kitchen and extended the metal antenna of his cordless phone.

A wave of relief rushed over me as I now realized they probably were not intent on robbing me or worse. As the phone rang, I took a mental inventory of my surroundings. In addition to the front door, there was a sliding door in the kitchen leading to the backyard, another door which I assumed led to the garage, and a handful of open windows which I would not hesitate to throw myself through if need be. I also had a general idea of the neighborhood I was in so if worst came to worst I could make a run for it and not find myself wandering aimlessly in unfamiliar territory. The various outcomes, all of them less than desirable, were streaming through my mind when I finally heard Janet's voice.

"Imo's. Can you please hold?"

Before I could say I'd rather not, she switched to the other line. If you think your computer's technical support representative takes a long time to answer, try waiting to speak to a live person while standing in a maniac's kitchen.

"Imo's. May I help you?" Oddly, just the thought of Janet's eyes was enough to lower the rapid beating of my frightened heart..

"Hey it's Todd. Can you please get Jack for me?"

"Is everything ok?" Janet asked. My anxiety was now beginning to reach a fevered pitch. I was calling for help, not to chit-chat."

"I just need to talk to Jack about this order… now!"

Janet must have sensed something in my voice and passed the urgency because I wasn't on hold for more than ten seconds before Jack got on the line.

"Jack, we have a problem with the order on Turnball Court," I said.

"What problem? There's no problem. I boxed that one myself," Jack replied defensively.

I didn't have the time or the patience to placate Jack's Sicilian ego.

"Well, the customer says it's wrong, and I think we need to send another one right away."

"Are they being jerks about it?" Jack asked, finally starting to get the picture.

I looked up at the man before answering. Although he was leaning against the kitchen counter watching me, I was fairly confident he hadn't heard what Jack had just asked me.

"I think so, yes," I responded as vaguely as I could.

That was the moment when all hell broke loose. What should have been one of many non-descript pizza deliveries that evening turned into a suburban middle-class version of a Liam Neeson film.

"Oh we're being jerks, huh?" blasted a voice from somewhere in the rear of the house. It seemed as if I was hearing it through both ears but from different channels.

Unbeknownst to me, one of the extras in this comedy of horrors had been listening in on my entire conversation with Jack via an extension in another room. He had heard Jack's question and, worse yet, the way I had chosen to answer.

At that very instant, I knew there was no more waiting for this situation would resolve itself. I didn't know what these guys were on or what they had in mind, but they were going to have to earn it from here on out. In a genuine situation like that, your adrenaline kicks in and it becomes fight or flight. It's the human instinct that I referred to in a previous chapter. Courage appears when you need it to the most, and that has allowed humans to survive for centuries. I needed to make an escape and make it right now.

The voices of all four of them became louder with a hint of agitation. I would describe it as confusion filled with angst. I can still hear the frantic shuffling of footsteps as the other three came running from the back of the house to the front. Soon I would be surrounded with nowhere to run. The man who had listened in on my call was trying to relay it to the man who had let me in the house in the first place. I'm sure he didn't catch every word, but he certainly got the gist and once again became totally focussed on me. With Jack still yelling through the receiver, I tossed the phone onto the kitchen table and saw it fall to the floor as I made a beeline for the front door.

Only one man made an attempt to grab me. I felt his hand brush the back of my shirt collar, but he couldn't get enough of a grip to stop me. Fortunately, the main door had remained open allowing me to plow right through the screen and out onto the porch.

Just as I had elected not to stop and politely open the screen door by the handle, I also didn't want to commit to the half second it would take to look behind me to see if I was being chased. The men could've been right on my heels or they could've been watching from the door and laughing. Either way, my sights were set on my little red car at the bottom of that long, steep driveway.

I'm sure the sight of me shuffling along, fighting gravity in an attempt not to slip on the wet pavement reflected anything but machismo. I didn't care. I reached the level surface of the street and jumped into the driver's seat of my car. My hands trembled as I started the ignition and pulled away. I was a good mile away before I could force myself to look into my rearview mirror. No one was following me. My Escort handled surprisingly well on the two-lane streets. Gradually I took my foot off of the accelerator and coasted down to the posted speed limit.

Once you realize that you are safely out of harm's way, you begin to consider all of the other possible outcomes and realize how lucky you are to be where you are. That encounter could've gotten to the point of becoming the top story on the evening news. Those four men could have easily overpowered me and thrown me into a makeshift dungeon in the basement. But what made me laugh out loud was the face that yes, they got a free pizza out of me. But the next morning they'd be writing a check for a new screen door.

You can never judge a book by its cover, and there are certainly plenty of wolves in sheep's clothing out there. The world can be a very creepy place and we need to keep our eyes open. Never again did I accept an invitation to come in out of the rain. I gained valuable *wisdom* from that *experience*.

I was pulling into the parking lot of the store when I noticed the second pizza still sitting next to me on the passenger seat. Sliding my hand inside the carrier to examine its warmth, I determined it was still at an acceptable temperature.

I had a choice to make. I could go directly back to Imo's where I knew my worried friends would hang on every word of my outrageous story, or I could try to salvage this delivery run. As is still so often the case, the words of my father came back to me:

If you're going to do a job, do it right.

I'm sure you can surmise what I ultimately chose to do. Realizing that it doesn't make a drop of sense to leave money on the table, I thumbed through the sauce-covered pages of my trusty *Thomas Guide* and got the directions for that next delivery. I had far exceeded the expected thirty-minute delivery window, but sometimes a smile and solemn apology go a long way with people.

I explained to the customer that one of our drivers had experienced a problem and we were a tiny bit behind schedule, but I wanted to take it upon myself to get her family's dinner to them as soon as I could. Not exactly a lie. More of a stretching of the truth.

And while my evening had provided enough excitement to last me a lifetime, the lovely woman standing before me looked as if she had enjoyed a relaxing day off and this Imo's pie was the icing on the cake for her. A special treat that perhaps the family only allowed themselves on special occasions. She handed me a twenty dollar bill and told me to keep the change. Quite a contrast to the previous home. I thanked her and wished her a goodnight as she gently closed the door.

There are two things I'd like for you to take away from my experience on Turnball Court. First, please never lose sight of the fact that there is an upside to any experience. It won't always be obvious, and it may come with a struggle, but receiving half a tip is better than getting no tip at all. By sticking to what was expected of me that evening, I was able to have my faith in mankind restored. The smile of the woman at the second home reminded me that not all people are creeps. And that reminder came at just the right time.

The second thing I'd like for you to remember is to please be patient the next time you have your dinner delivered. Allow yourself to slow down a little. This I-Need-It-Yesterday society we now find ourselves living in isn't the way life is supposed to be. Enjoy the person you are with and enjoy, too, those times where you have your solitude. So what if your pizza is a few minutes late? Cut that delivery kid some slack. Who knows? He may have just run full speed through a screen door.

CHAPTER 11

No Photography in the White House

The funny thing about working in television is you often forget that there are people watching. I believe I speak on behalf of many stage managers, camera operators, directors, sound and lighting technicians, makeup artists, and even producers when I say this. It's very easy to get caught up in all that is happening on set and the fact that people at home actually make time in their busy day to sit down and watch our finished product is extremely gratifying.

A live performances is an entirely different beast than a recorded show. The feedback you receive from a stage production is immediate. Many times I can hear the sound of a charged-up audience from backstage-sometimes from as far away as my dressing room. You will know then and there if what you're doing is to their liking.

We also receive valuable data prior to showtime in the form of a ticket count that tells us what size audience to expect that night. During the performance, the wave of applause serves as an indication of approval. Nothing compares to the rush that comes from knowing something special has just taken place and everyone was in on the moment. You can't touch that feeling of knowing that things are working, and that feeling stays with you you long after the curtain comes down and the lights have gone out.

TV is much different. The gratification is certainly there, but is often delayed weeks or even months. I recall catching a rerun of a 2003 episode of *Whammy!: The All New Press Your Luck* while waiting for my car to be serviced at a Jiffy Lube and being able to remember the dinner I had at Dan Tana's the evening of the taping. There have also been moments much more recently where I've been watching *Family Game Night* and couldn't even remember the answers to the questions I was asking on screen. Many times I'd be dressed in a Santa outfit next to a giant tree covered in basketball-sized ornaments for a Christmas show we were taping in the middle of June. The concept of time is nonexistent in the world of television, and it can be very confusing.

Obviously people do watch the shows we create. This is shown by the fact that television ratings drive revenue. It's big business. People tune in to watch the hot shows and the advertising dollars come flowing in. Shows that aren't cutting the mustard go by the wayside. There was one particular show that I was involved in that I believed was going to be quite successful had a shot to go the distance.

Made in the USA premiered on the USA Network in September of 2005 and featured inventors and entrepreneurs from around the country who were competing to win a contract to market their product on Home Shopping Network. I felt, as did the creators, that presenting the viewing audience with all access view of the process of bringing a product to the marketplace combined with the passion and drive of these hungry contestants would make for compelling television. I was wrong. The ratings could be described as mediocre at best and the show couldn't hold on.

We had grossly misjudged what viewers wanted and our season came to a screeching halt with a finale that was aired only on the Internet.

Though not always an accurate depiction of the true picture, ratings are what those of us in the television industry live and die by. Viewers have been very kind to me throughout my career and though I have had a couple of misses with *Made in the USA* and FOX's *Performing As...*, I am grateful for the continued success of *Whammy!* and for the place in history *Family Game Night* was able to carve out with just over 100 episodes. But the biggest surprise of my now twenty-plus years on television has been the sustainability of a show I was a part of before the turn of the century.

Hollywood Showdown was my debut into the world of game shows. Before big, loud programs like *Deal or No Deal* came along, the traditional style of game show was still pulling an impressive share of the ratings. *Showdown* was a consistent winner for GSN for nearly three years before the new regime of network executives decided to pull the plug in order to make room for a fresh lineup of original programming.

Created and produced by Sande Stewart, a man who would quickly become a driving force in my development as a game show host, *Hollywood Showdown* was a charmingly simple concept. Two contestants stood on either side of me at a podium placed under the shade neon palm trees. I asked a multiple choice question and the first player to buzz in with the correct answer received a point. The first player to get three points would move on to the next round and face a new player until we had the day's champion. That lucky man or woman would join me in the Box Office round to answer more pop culture trivia questions in hopes of walking away with a sizable amount of money and returning the next day to play again.

Sande knew what worked. Together with his father Bob, he had developed such iconic shows as *To Tell the Truth*, *Password*, and *The $25,000 Pyramid*. Bob even had a hand in the creation of *The Price is Right*. For many years, the father and son duo had their fingers on the pulse of the American television viewer, and it was clear to them that audiences loved the basics. Sande once confided in me that the key to a great game show is getting the audience at home to talk back to their television within the first minute of the broadcast. *Price* certainly does that, and *Hollywood Showdown* did it too.

We shot 65 episodes during *Showdown*'s first season and got word that we'd received a pick-up for a second season before taking our hiatus. As a promotional tool, the network sent me out on a cross country contestant search during the off months. The search would require me to host a scaled down version of our show in malls in some of the larger television markets. Philadelphia, San Antonio, Miami, Washington, D.C., and Chicago were just a few of the cities on the schedule and GSN generously offered to compensate me with Sony products rather than cash. When the mini-tour was over, we had acquired massive amounts of exposure in some key areas, and I had furnished my home with the latest model televisions, camcorders, stereos, and computers.

I had also met viewers face-to-face which, as I knew from my time on the radio, is the best way to establish a loyal fan base. Shake one person's hand and you might as well be shaking the hands of all of her friends. Be courteous enough to spend five minutes with someone who enjoys what you do and they will share that experience with everyone they know.

The type of personal interaction that I experienced on the contestant search gives a performer a chance to hear firsthand what is working with a particular show and what isn't. Fans are not afraid to tell you the truth. They are entitled to an opinion, and it is in your best interest to pay it a fair amount of attention. Remember, the audience is your boss and any type of demographic analysis is beneficial.

Appearing live is also a wonderful way to meet new and interesting people with whom you may form friendships. Taking the time to really listen to someone's story is as fascinating as getting lost within the pages of a good book. Like Mr. Barker always says, everyone has a story. One man in particular who came to see me during a stop at The National Mall in Washington, DC, stands out in my mind as an all time favorite.

For the sake of his personal and professional privacy, we shall call him Steve. In his early to mid-fifties and standing just shy of six feet tall, Steve's presence was felt long before he made his way to our makeshift stage centrally located in the mall's atrium. Like everyone else who was waiting patiently in line, Steve was hoping to win a chance to be flown to California and be a contestant on *Hollywood Showdown*. Had he simply shown up at one of the L.A. casting calls I'm sure the contestant coordinators would have selected him in a blink of an eye. With his tailored suit and perfect posture, he had the look of a man in charge. In fact, he was dressed better than I was.

After what must have been a forty-five minute to an hour long wait, it was finally Steve's turn to join me on the platform. His handshake was firm, like that of a world leader or CEO. His demeanor was calm and focused. After greeting his opponent, a female college student who looked as if she just stumbled upon our event after picking up a new skirt at American Eagle, Steve placed his left hand behind his back, his right hand on the red buzzer, and waited for me to ask the first question.

"Tell me which member of the Rat Pack visited Archie Bunker and his…"

Buzz. Not only did I not need to give the choices for the answer, I hadn't even completed the question. The young lady looked at Steve and then to me with a face that read defeat.

"Yes, Steve?"

"Sammy Davis, Jr."

"Sammy Davis, Jr. is correct," I informed the audience. In the interest of time, the live version of *Showdown* only required players to get two out three answers correct as opposed to being the first to give three correct answers on television. Steve was well on his way. "One more correct answer and you move on to the next round."

Steve reassumed his position and, with his head bowed and eyes closed, prepared for the next question.

"Who was the fist person to appear on the cover of *Rolling Stone*? Was it, A) Elvis Presley, B) John Lennon, or C) Bob Dylan?"

Both contestants weighed the options for a split second before buzzing in at the exact same moment. No one knew who had the upper hand so the crowd looked to me for a decision. There was an opportunity to add some drama here. I had a chance to create something out of nothing and show these Saturday afternoon shoppers how we do things in Gameshow Land. Assuming the odds were in Steve's favor, I decided to let the moment simmer by calling on the young woman first.

"Yes, Lisa."

Her hesitation revealed her uncertainty. She was going to toss out a guess, but with a one in three shot she could very likely tie the game up and force Steve to the third and final question. She was the underdog. The dark horse. And we all held our breath waiting for her final answer.

"Well, my mom is a huge fan, so I'm just going to take a guess…is it Elvis?" The audience gasped while Steve buzzed in to bring it home.

"No, I'm sorry, it isn't Elvis. Steve, you could win the round with the correct answer." In classic host form, I repeated the question. "Who was the first person to appear on the cover of *Rolling Stone?*"

"Todd, I believe it was John Lennon. If I recall, he was dressed in a full military uniform from the set of a movie he was working on."

"You're absolutely right! The movie was *How I Won The War* and you are one step closer to joining us in Hollywood. Congratulations!"

As it turns out, Steve winning the trip to Los Angeles was not to be. It should come as no surprise that some of the contestants who showed up for our events really knew their stuff and came to ready to play. People have a tendency to bring their A game when there are prizes and bundles of cash at stake. Although Steve did well, we had to say goodbye to him in the third round.

Depending on the size of the crowd that came out, a contestant search could last anywhere from ninety minutes to more than three hours. I never even considered leaving before every person who wanted to play had that chance, but I would take breaks occasionally and let a local radio or television personality hand out t-shirts or CDs while I rested my feet and voice. It was during one of these timeouts that Steve approached me and gave me his business card.

"Todd, I really had a great time. It was a pleasure meeting you. I just want to give you my information. If you would ever like a private tour of the White House, please don't hesitate to call me."

A private tour of the White House? Did I hear him correctly? I looked down at the card I'd been handed and, sure enough, my new friend Steve was with The United States Secret Service.

"Wow," I said. "The Secret Service? The fancy suits, sunglasses, earpieces. That must be an exciting gig."

"Oh, it certainly is. But I've really always wanted to be a game show host." We both laughed. "I'm serious about my invitation. I don't know how long you'll be in town, but the offer stands."

I've always been intrigued by the power and secrecy that shrouds our Commander in Chief. Like many Americans, I had heard the rumors of a secret tunnel that was accessible by a trap door under the desk in the Oval Office. I had witnessed the sheer bravery of agent Clint Hill who, while assigned to Jackie Kennedy's detail, attempted to cover JFK's body with his own after the first shot was fired in Dallas on November 22, 1963. I envied the integrity these men and women must demonstrate in all areas of their lives to even be considered for a position on this elite protective force. And now a member of that same squad was standing before me and offering to take me where so few have the occasion to go.

It just so happens that Silver had chosen to join me on this particular leg of the tour. Born and raised just outside of our nation's capital, her parents still lived in the area. The visit would allow her to break away from the busy life of an E! producer and enjoy some much-needed family time. We were still in the early stages of our relationship and what better way to impress the woman you're crazy about than to surprise her with a late night visit to the White House?

Steve had graciously offered to let me bring a few friends along so we extended the invitation to Silver's mother, the publicist who had taken such good care of me on the trips, and a well-known Hollywood contestant coordinator who was impossible to shake. Hanging out with this particular individual often proved to be exhausting as she talked non-stop and wanted to stop and take pictures of everything she saw from water fountains outside of the hotel to whatever new tie I happened to be wearing, but because we were all staying at the same hotel and had been dining together since the search began, it would have been more trouble than it was worth to try and keep this excursion a secret. Inviting her felt like the right thing to do at the time.

Steve and I made arrangements to meet the following evening. It would be our final night in DC, and I wanted it to be special for Silver. When I presented Steve's offer to her, she couldn't believe it. Growing up in such a historic city exposes one to more history than those of us who grew up in other regions may ever get to experience. The Lincoln Memorial, the Washington Monument, and Arlington National Cemetery are moving reminders of what a significant role America has played in history and residents of DC and the surrounding parts of Virginia are fortunate enough to drive by them on a daily basis. Tourists travel from thousands of miles away just to look at the White House from afar and here we were preparing to take a stroll inside.

Silver, her mother, the publicist Julia, our contestant coordinator, and I gathered in the lobby of The George Hotel at 7 p.m.. Our plan was to have a quick dinner before meeting Steve at the southeast gate of the White House at 9. By then, Steve assured us, the majority of office workers would be gone and the public tours would have ended for the day. "Being there at that time of night allows you to get a feel for how powerful of a place it is," Steve said. Apparently the man took great pride in his country and his duty, and I'll admit it rubbed off on me.

Silver, her mother, and I took one taxi while the other two ladies followed in another. If our driver thought it odd that were asking to be dropped off outside the president's home so late at night, he didn't mention it. I could sense the excitement being felt by everyone in our party. None of us had ever done anything remotely like this. I've been all around the world and enjoyed some unique encounters, but this topped them all.

As promised, and as one would expect from a Secret Service agent, Steve was waiting for us at the gate promptly at 9 o'clock. The moment became real when he said, "Ladies and Gentleman, welcome to the White House." At that point, I knew it was really going to happen. People over-promise and under-deliver all the time, and I suppose the skeptic in me was prepared for Steve not to be there when we pulled up or have a reason why the tour wasn't going to be possible. But neither of those things happened. We were at the White House and we were going in.

"But," Steve said, interrupting the dialogue in my head. "I do need to inform you that President and Mrs. Clinton *are* in residence so there can be no photography of any kind. And if I suddenly instruct you to follow me you are to do so immediately. Is that understood?"

I felt like a child being warned by a parent. *Behave yourself in here or we're not stopping for ice cream on the way home*. We all nodded our acceptance of the terms he had so forcefully laid before us. The tone of his voice was not disciplinary. Instead, it showed how special what we were about to do really was. We weren't jumping the line to ride Space Mountain at DisneyLand; we were being allowed to walk through the back door of the home of the most powerful person in the free world.

As we made our up the driveway, Steve explained that Thomas Jefferson was the first president to offer tours of the White House to the public. He believed that it really belonged to the American people and should not be limited to a few select individuals. But we felt privileged and fortunate to be in the company of this man who's duty it was to protect this sacred institution. And wherever he led we would follow.

"Many visitors enjoy seeing the press room. Would you like to stop there before we head to the Oval Office?"

The James S. Brady Press Briefing Room is much, much smaller than it appears on CNN, but it is unmistakable, nonetheless. Located in the West Wing, it is the all-to-familiar setting of the Press Secretary's daily address to the media and where every American has watched president after president address the nation. The room was constructed in 1970 by order of President Nixon to accommodate the growing demand for television coverage of White House business. It's close proximity allows officials to issue statements to the press promptly.

My group was informed that this would be the only location on our tour where we would be allowed to pull out our cameras. One by one we were allowed to step carefully behind the famous podium and have our photos taken. I let Silver go first, then her mother. When it was my turn, I opted to pose as if I was delivering a speech. A strange sensation came over me as I placed my hands on either side of the wooden lectern; I could sense the power of the presidency. My mind took me somewhere other than on that stage as I imagined the men who had stood on that very spot and the responsibilities that had fallen upon their shoulders. The decisions that were made through the door just to my right impacted millions of people and shaped the way we lived our lives for generations to come. It was a forceful and moving sensation that I've never forgotten.

The next and final stop on our behind-the-scenes adventure would be the Oval Office. It is important to note that I am a student of power and influence. The ways in which persuasion and control shape our culture are enchanting to me. We seem to have been molded to rely on a total stranger to lead us and have a blind trust that he or she will care for our needs and wants. Some societies look to royalty, others to elected officials, some have no choice in leadership, but whatever the case of a particular land, there is always a figurehead that represents the final word. In the United States, that man was Bill Clinton and I was steps away from where he ruled the nation.

The scandal involving President Clinton and Monica Lewinsky, an intern with whom he was alleged to have had an extramarital affair, was still very much in the news at the time of our visit to the White House. The very hallway through which I now walked was the same hallway Monica would have taken to visit the president. The door through which I would soon pass was the same one they closed to ensure their privacy. It was a hallway rich in history, steeped in importance, and dripping with impropriety.

I recall the walls being white and lined with wooden baseboards. The carpet was a combination of primary colors set against heavy oak furniture producing a professional yet historic setting. Mirrors and landscape paintings were hung evenly down the hallway, and wall tables were decorated with lovely arrangements of fresh flowers.

Click. Click. Click. The sound of the camera and the reflection of its flash in the mirrors brought the entire group to a halt. Steve spun around on his heels.

"Please, no cameras. Let me remind you that they are absolutely prohibited in this part of the building."

Already I was regretting asking the contestant coordinator to join us. Silver attempted to calm me with a look, but I felt her actions were reflecting poorly on me. In addition to the reprimand issued by Steve, I had personally asked her to please put her camera in her purse and leave it there until we were through with the tour. She giggled with embarrassment and pretended to wave off the warning.

We continued on. As we rounded the final corner of the long corridor, a dreamlike image appeared before us. I choose to call it an image because it held the magnificence of a painting or a photograph one would see on the cover of *Time*. We had arrived at the Oval Office.

Peering through the northwest door, my eyes went straight to the infamous desk where the likes of JFK, Truman, Eisenhower, Roosevelt, and Reagan presided over their empires. This was the desk upon which legislation was signed and at which treaties were reached. Behind the desk were the giant picture windows through which some of history's most powerful minds gazed in deep thought, pondering America's tomorrows.

I noticed, too, the royal blue rug emblazoned with the gold presidential seal and on it the perfectly arranged couches where discussions of the highest order were held. I closed my eyes and imagined the heated debates between the men and women seated on those very cushions, possibly as recently as that very afternoon.

My daydreaming came to an abrupt end when Steve suddenly informed us that we needed to back away from the doorway immediately. There was no alarm in his voice. Just the same calm and cool he had demonstrated at the mall. He was pure focus and all business as he stood in front of us like a human shield.

Silver saw him first. I followed her stunned gaze to the window and out toward the direction of the Rose Garden. I recall the others in the group gasping, *"Oh my God!"* and *"He's right there."*

And there he was. Dressed in a white bathrobe and being accompanied to the White House pool by two of Steve's fellow agents, either one of whom would dive in front of a bullet to save that man regardless of people said about him in the newspapers. All that separated me from President Bill Clinton, one of the most beloved leaders in history, were a couple of couches and some window panes.

One might assume that the president wouldn't be too pleased to walk past his office window late at night and see a herd of strangers meddling about his private quarters, but he just gave us that classic Clinton smile and a quick wave before continuing down the pathway.

Click. Click. Click.

Again our contestant coordinator had blatantly disobeyed the one simple instruction we'd been given.

"There is no photography in the White House!"

But she couldn't help herself and frankly who could blame her? I can understand getting swept up in such a moment, but it was the fact that she was so unashamed in her actions that made me want to scream with rage. Though Steve clearly had no intention of putting his job at risk for the sake of a game show host and his picture-obsessed posse, to expect a woman who snaps photos of strangers on bicycles would pass up a picture of the president in his swimming trunks is unrealistic.

We had seen far more than we expected to see and done far more than we ever expected to do on a Sunday night in Washington. Steve had gifted us an experience we'd all be talking about for years to come. I stopped at the guard gate and turned to take one more mental picture of where we had just been while everyone thanked Steve for his time, trouble, and generosity. When Silver's mother finished hugging him, I approached with my hand out.

"I can't thank you enough, Steve. This has really been incredible," I said. "And I'm sorry about…," pointing over my shoulder at you-know-who.

"Don't mention it. It happens all the time," he said. "I'm really glad you all could make it." We shook hands again before I joined my lady friends on the other side of the gates.

Steve called my name as we were hailing the taxis at the top of the waiting line. I turned around to see him waving me over for a moment of privacy.

"Some of the boys are going shooting at our private range tomorrow. You're welcome to join us."

If only I had booked a later flight back to Hollywood.

CHAPTER 12

Twenty Years Too Late

Chuck Barris is a game show pioneer. Known primarily as the lovable host of *The Gong Show*, Chuck did much more for the genre than just wear silly hats and introduce Gene Gene the Dancing Machine. He also created *The Dating Game* (one of only two game shows I appeared on as a contestant), *3's a Crowd*, *Treasure Hunt*, and *The Newlywed Game*. In addition, he authored the 1952 Freddy Cannon hit "Palisade's Park" which went to #3 on the Billboard Hot 100 chart.

In 2002, Chuck wrote his autobiography *Confessions of a Dangerous Mind*, in which he alluded to being a CIA agent operating under the disguise of a game show producer. The book created so much buzz that it was made into a major motion picture and starred some of the biggest names in the industry: Julia Roberts, Drew Barrymore, and George Clooney, who also directed the film.

Mr. Barris was kind enough to offer invitations to the Hollywood premiere of his movie to those of us whom he believed to be the future of game shows. Never before had I been asked to attend such an event as a guest. I had covered many star-studded premieres for E!, but on this night I would be the interviewee on the red carpet rather than the interviewer. The evening was sure to be a display of Tinseltown at its finest. Studios pull out all the stops at these events in hopes of getting as much coverage as possible for the movie, and with the entire cast slated to make an appearance, there would no doubt be cameras flashing from every angle.

GSN suggested the other invited hosts and I arrive as a package deal to provide a better photo opportunity for the many outlets that would be present. I was joined by former MTV VJ Kennedy, Mark L. Walberg of *Russian Roulette*, and Mr. Two-and-Two himself, Chuck Woolery, who was hosting *Lingo* at the time.

One could hear the grunts of disappointment from the hoards of spectators lining the streets when our limousine pulled up and out climbed a handful of faces from basic cable, but it didn't dampen our enthusiasm. For that one special night, we were part of the big time and nothing was going to take that away from us.

As my fellow hosts and I sauntered down the red carpet among some of the film's writers and producers, I was repeatedly asked by the press why I believed Chuck Barris was so relatable to so many generations of fans. Though a generic question, my answer was tight and bright: because with Chuck Barris, you know exactly what you are going to get, and you like it. He's funny. He's charming. He teeters on the blue side of things. And he makes you enjoy watching television.

Reporter after reporter nodded and thanked me for my answer. As an interviewer myself, I know that a well-delivered soundbite makes one's job easy. They could take my clip and air it as is. No editing required. And that's exactly what happened. As shows like *Entertainment Tonight* and *Access Hollywood* aired footage of the glamorous Julia and George the heart-throb, there too was I with my little snippet saying what needed to be said.

Experiencing the Hollywood hoopla of just one movie premier made it easy for me to understand why so many stars become reclusive. The screaming fans, publicists tugging at your sleeves, and a barrage cameras in your face can be daunting if you're not able to find a way to escape from it. I've never reached a degree of recognition where I haven't been able to enjoy a pizza with my kids or a relaxing walk on the beach with my dog without paparazzi snapping pictures of my bad side. Stopping to take a photo in an airport is flattering, but the life of an A-lister is something I will never fully comprehend. But it does come with some upsides, too.

Let's put the money and fame aside for the time being. The entertainment industry is plush with special perks. The adoration of fans and traveling by private jet is enough to make anyone salivate with envy. But one of the greatest benefits I've personally encountered at my level is the ability to meet some of the most creative people alive. They are writers, musicians, and artists, that I find alluring because they live for, and are fully committed to, their crafts. Whether it results in a deep friendship that lasts over a span of many years or a fleeting chat, much can be taken away from these relationships and encounters. One, solitary sentence from Chuck Barris let me know I was on the right path with my crazy dreams.

The premiere was all about him. In a sense, it was a tribute to all he had given us through his many projects. Though the night was focused on his film, the film focused on his life. *Confessions of a Dangerous Mind* may be an admission of one man's secret life, or it may be purely fictional. The intrigue lies in the not knowing. But one thing I can tell you for certain is that Chuck knows game shows and game show hosts.

Getting close enough to speak to him was going to be difficult. The publicists had arranged for Chuck to arrive just as the film's stars were pulling up. There would be hundreds of photographs of them hugging and laughing as if they were the best of friends and the making of this picture had been the climax of all of their careers. Chuck would be asked if he really was a spy and he'd dance around the question to add to the mystery. But there would come a moment at some point in the evening where I'd be able to say hello. I could feel it. Sooner or later he would wander into a quiet corner or want to get a drink at the bar. And when that time came I would pounce.

That moment presented itself at the end of the carpet where everyone was preparing to enter the theater to watch the movie. Inside there would only be invited guests. The press did not have access to the theater nor did they particularly want it. They had only come for the pictures and the video and now they needed to rush back to their editing suites. The night had gone from a ten on the energy meter to a weakened six as even a few of the major stars continued straight through the theater and out the back door to their awaiting cars. They had already seen the final cut and had no intention of remaining in their designer garbs any longer than was absolutely needed. The premier was just part of the job, and once the required smiles and waves had been dished out it was time for them to clock out.

Chuck was shaking a few hands and receiving some pats on the back when I summoned the nerve to approach him. I waited at a respectful distance, careful not to let anyone bump me out of the way or steal his attention, and when it was my turn, I introduced myself with a smile. As I did so, I was reminded of how much my mother enjoyed watching *The Gong Show*. Here was the man that not only made me feel like a star on this magical California evening, but who had brought the most special lady in my life so much joy back when she was a stay-at-home mom with two young boys. The show must have served as a much-deserved break from her busy and thankless days.

"Chuck, I just want to introduce myself. My name is Todd Newton. I host a game show called *Whammy!* on GSN." It was my elevator introduction.

"Oh sure, Todd. Very nice to meet you."

I was hoping he'd clap at the end of every sentence the way he always did on television, but he didn't. I'd read somewhere that the clapping was a nervous habit of his brought about by being on television. As the producer of *The Gong Show*, Chuck was never able to find a host that the network would approve of. Finally, after auditioning every emcee in town, the higher-ups told him he should host the show himself. Although he was never quite comfortable in the role, he did what he had to do to keep the show on the air and became a star as a result. Seeing his hands resting comfortably at his side, I had to assume that I wasn't making him as nervous as he was making me.

"I just want to thank you for inviting me tonight and to ask if you might have time for me to buy you lunch while you're in town. I'd love to get your thoughts on my hosting."

I realized that I was swinging for the fences with my request, but all he could say was no. You don't improve at anything without a little help from others, and I believe in tapping into the experience of those who have mastered whatever it is you're pursuing. If he refused, I would just return to my friends and enjoy the rest of the night. But if his answer was yes, it would mean the opportunity to sit at the feet of a master.

Chuck politely informed me that he was scheduled to return to his home in France the following day. What I didn't tell him for fear of coming across as pathetic was that I would've gladly purchased a full fare ticket on the five thousand mile flight if it meant I'd be under his tutelage.

"But I've seen your stuff," he continued. "And I gotta tell ya, I think you came along twenty years too late. If you'd been around in the seventies, you'd have been right up there with the best of them."

Did Chuck Barris truly work a spy and did he really do all that he claimed to have done in his book? If so, then he has, no doubt, been trained to read people. He would be able to tell what others are thinking by their breathing patterns and the way their bodies are postured. He would have the ability to interpret what we are feeling not by the words we choose, but by the way we choose to say them. In my heart, I hope what he wrote is indeed the truth because then he would know what I felt when he said those words to me.

"Thank you, Chuck. Thanks a lot," is all I had for him. He shook my hand and reached up to hit me on my right shoulder.

I've never focused on trying to be better than anyone else. My only competition is with myself. I want to outdo the father, the man, and the host I was yesterday. I don't need to be labeled as the best host ever; I just need to be the best host I can be. And though I may have been a couple of decades tardy to the party, I'm still here as loud and proud as they come. And I have no plans on leaving anytime soon.

Afterword

"Just remember, you're the icing. Not the whole cake."

That peril of wisdom was passed on to me by *The Newlywed Game* legend, Bob Eubanks backstage at NBC's *Today*. I always found Bob to be a real gentleman and no one can throw an innocent look to the camera the way he did for so many years. Bob and I were in New York to appear on *Today* as part of a special week honoring game show hosts. I was honored to represent *Whammy!* alongside Bob, Bob Barker, Monty Hall of *Let's Make A Deal*, and Peter Marshall of *Hollywood Squares*. It was a significant moment for me in that I was able to share with Al Roker how each of these men had influenced me throughout my career. Rarely do we get to thank those who have meant something to us along the way. When such an opportunity is presented we can't let it slip by.

Earlier that year Bob had been gracious enough to formally introduce me to the audience of a lottery game show I would be taking over from him. In 2004, *Instant Millionaire* was slated to replace a show Bob had been hosting for many years called *Powerball: The Game Show.*

During his sign off in the final episode, he informed viewers that the new version would be hosted by a "wonderfully talented young man named Todd Newton," and he encouraged them to tune in the following week. It was a display of professional generosity that is not often seen in show business, and it certainly did not go unnoticed by me.

The host of any event serves as the ringleader, but he or she is far from being the entire circus. Johnny Carson once said during an interview that he became a star by allowing the real stars to shine. I find that incredibly admirable and often repeat those words to myself when I feel that urge to grab hold of the limelight and keep it all for myself.

Hosting is my craft as well as my passion and I believe in continuously working to improve at it. I believe in the "University of Doin' It", because doing it is all I've ever done. Friction creates fire and every event I am fortunate enough to be a part of allows me to grow by exploring new stage movements, ways to interact with the crowd as a whole, and interview techniques.

More so than with other occupations, a host is what I'm known *as* more so than what I'm known *for*. It has become more of a label than a job title, and that is exactly why I've trademarked The Host with the Most®. I love that handle. In fact, I love it so very deeply that I now I own it, figuratively and literally. As an extreme showing of commitment, I also had those four words tattooed on my right arm. They are mine. Forever.

With *Age* comes *Wisdom* through *Experience*. Wisdom and experience have shown me time and again that hosting, whether it be calling bingo at a nursing home or awarding cash and prizes on a popular television game show, is built upon a cornerstone. That cornerstone is a connection with your audience, viewer, or customer. Hosting, presenting, emceeing are all even more cerebral than acting which focuses primarily on stirring up emotion. You feel as if you really know your favorite hosts, and so it should be. There is a relationship present. You can envision them driving, eating, and sleeping. You can even predict how they will react and what they will say in certain situations. It is comfort food for the mind that makes us feel as if we're spending time with a friend. And that feeling is justified by the fact that, though slightly enhanced for your entertainment pleasure, what you are being given is the real person. If it's an artificial facade you're looking for in a companion, I suggest you date a model.

My approach to hosting experienced a significant transformation with the birth of my children. When they entered the world life immediately became richer. Parents and grandparents will certainly understand what I mean when I say the world becomes more vibrant and whole when kids are around. I was nearly taken aback by how I suddenly began to view things as eventful as holidays and as routine as riding a bike through the eyes of my son and daughter. I once again saw the magic in everything thanks to the both of them and chose to apply this newly discovered logic to my style of hosting.

When I share a stage with a contestant or interview a guest, I am fully aware that it may be a once in a lifetime moment for that person. I am also aware of how fortunate I am for getting to do what I do for a living. I travel to fascinating and majestic locations. I perform in luxury resorts and on the stages of some of the most ornate theaters in America. I share meals and conversation with great minds. And I get to do it all with the love and support of my precious family.

Believe me, I am thankful beyond belief for all that I get to experience. But when I am truly in the moment with someone, I make a conscious effort to experience it from their point of view. It's their day, not mine.

Just as I now look forward to Christmas more than I ever have at any other point in my life because I feel such joy from watching my children rip open their presents, I cannot wait to meet the next contestant and share that special day with them. This perspective on my craft allows me to maintain a level of freshness and makes each game or interview as unique as the person I'm standing alongside. They are the boss and I owe it to them to make our time together as special as possible.

As you can see, The Host with the Most® is more than just a catchy phrase to me. It is a reflection of the respect and appreciation I have for my occupation. No one has the right to downplay or belittle what you do to feed your family. There is no room in today's world for jealousy or pettiness. It will only slow you down and keep you from reaching your full potential.

I'm certain that there is no shortage of people who would gladly trade positions with you regardless of what it is you do for a living. Bask in the knowledge that you are living someone's dream.

If your current lot in life is unfulfilling, I encourage you to explore new horizons. Maximize your free time to educate yourself and develop new skills in areas that interest you. For instance, I am obsessed with the world of real estate. The negotiation of high dollar deals and the feeling of permanence that comes with the purchase of a new home invigorate me and I have immersed myself in that space with the development of Newton Luxury Realty.

Success is achievable for you if you focus on enhancing your strengths and pursue something that really turns you on. Remember, it will never feel like work if you love what it is you're waking up to do. There is no substitute for vim, vigor, and vitality.

I will never stand before you and boast of being the most handsome man on television, though it may very well be true. Please do not look for me to win the Nobel Peace Price anytime soon. And chances are you won't bump into me at your next MENSA meeting. But if you're looking to meet the host with the most respect for what he does, the most love in his heart for his family, and the most gratitude toward those of you who join me on the air everywhere, I believe you've found him.

Made in the USA
San Bernardino, CA
27 December 2016